ANCHOR BOOKS

ANCHOR POETS 1995

First published in Great Britain in 1995 by
ANCHOR BOOKS
1-2 Wainman Road, Woodston,
Peterborough, PE2 7BU

HB ISBN 1 85930 274 2
SB ISBN 1 85930 279 3

Foreword

Anchor Books is a small press, established in 1992, with the aim of promoting readable poetry to as wide an audience as possible.

We hope to establish an outlet for writers of poetry who may have struggled to see their work in print.

The poems presented here have been selected from many entries. Editing proved to be a difficult and daunting task and as the Editor, the final selection was mine.

The poems chosen represent a cross-section of styles and content. They have been sent from all over the world, written by young and old alike, united in the passion for writing poetry.

I trust this selection will delight and please the authors and all those who enjoy reading poetry.

Andrew Head
Editor

CONTENTS

REVERIE

I love to walk by the seashore,
And feel the wind in my hair,
To dangle my toes in the rippling waves,
Without a thought or a care.

I love to walk by the seashore,
And gaze at the mighty ocean,
To feel the spray as the zephyrs blow,
The waves in perpetual motion.

I love to walk by the seashore,
And hear the sound of the gull,
As it dips and dives on the tempest,
Floating peacefully when there's a lull.

I love to walk by the seashore,
As the sun sinks into the west,
Casting its shadows of evening abroad,
This time of the day I love best.

Pat Fisher

ODE TO OWNERS

Whilst I appreciate dogs must pooh
as of course do me and you,
If yours does - there is a bin
So please pick it up and put it in!

Zena Giles

1

OUR STRUGGLE LEAVES A MARK

The way was hard with
danger near by, but still I
struggle on. There are lots of
dreams and many themes,
that are sad and gay,
glistening in the heart.

As I climb up the mountain,
it's higher than a fountain
and yet I still struggle on.
Days pass by and months
go by, but never feel down
in the dumps. For we struggled
hard and fought hard.
With our marks right
here to show it.

Joseph Sagnia

UNTITLED

Baby
I try to see
things through your eyes.

But I can't seem to see
those things through my eyes.

Even when I shut mine
all I see is your disguise.

Hiding those things
which you say are true
but are only lies.

A Pearce

FANTASY AND REALITY

I love the approach to Christmas
When the streets are all aglow
Sleigh bells tinkling in the distance
On a silent carpet of snow
When the berries are on the holly
And the tinsel's on the tree
When twilight drops on candle-lit shops
That's the favourite time for me.

The bells sparkling from the churches
Children whispering in the choir
Carols seeping through our curtains
Apple logs crackling on the fire
Father playing on the piano
The family gathering round
With cheerful voice we all rejoice
A warm and a wondrous sound.

But December's dull and murky
For a spurious spending spree
And the cat's just mauled the turkey
While the dog's 'christened' the tree
And it's mayhem down at Tesco's
They're all stocking up for a siege
While here indoors it's all-out war
And the holly's been grabbed by thieves.

And the streets are damp and dirty
Peddling recycled Status Quo
And all we're fed are Spielburgers
And another remake of 'Dr No'
Father watches tired old war films
The sprogs their screeching VDUs
And for half a week on Oxford Street
Mother happily sits and queues.

J J Crossley

CONTRASTS

I well recall a day so fine
When all the world was really mine.
I had a chance to get away
Albeit only for a day,
With heavens blue, no chance of rain
So, off I went upon a train
That took me at a thrilling pace
Towards a far-off seaside place.
Once there, a long walk by the sea.
Seagulls flying over me.
Swooping low, then soaring high.
Like ballet dancers in the sky
Water, lapping at my feet
Like angel's kisses, such a treat.
'Twas like a jewel in my crown
For one escaping from a town.
Where smoky chimneys, buildings high
Shut out the view and sun and sky.
The contrasts made me stop and pray
And thank God for my perfect day.

M I Grove

A TRYER

Game has started, you play the field.
Mistakes are made, you never yield.
You do you're best, the game gets rough,
Scores are made, one must get tough.
The ball you have, you run the pitch,
You've scored again without a hitch.
there's heavy sweat upon your brow,
Rest you need, but not just now.
Cheers are heard from the happy crowd,
The team has won we feel so proud.

Glad Davies

4

SAND BETWEEN ME TOES

Sun, sea, sand and rich blue sky,
They attract the crowds in droves.
But there is one thing that I abhor,
That's sand between me toes.

I love to join the bustling crowds,
And strip off all my clothes.
to lie and bathe the whole day long,
With sand between me toes.

I never venture beyond my towel,
To watch the puppet shows.
I'll sit here safely so I'll not get,
Some sand between me toes.

I would love to dip in the sea,
Yet still one thing gets up my nose,
I cannot wander from this spot,
As sand will get in me toes.

And now the day draws to a close,
I'll return home now I suppose.
I reach the path and you'll never guess,
Sand is in me toes.

J A Iliff

MY BEST FRIEND MY TEDDY BEAR

He's really rather quaint and cute.
As he sits on my bedroom chair
one of my very dearest friends
My little teddy bear.

I know he's watching over me
at night when I'm asleep
I couldn't bear to part with him
as my love for him is so deep.

On special days and birthdays
he wears a nice new bow
he really knows that he's the tops
the little so and so.

He really has seen better days
for he's nearly as old as me
I've reached the age of seventy-eight
and I've had him since I was three.

He's been through the war the poor little thing
His ears are twisted and funny
a missing eye and a cut on his nose
and a very odd patch on his tummy.

So he's really quite threadbare by now
through hugging him so very tight
I'd die if anything happened to him
so when I go to bed at night
I hug and cuddle him and say
Night, night little teddy bear night, night.

Eileen Neal

LIFE IN THE NINETIES

Bosses in your boardrooms grand
I wonder, do you really understand
The misery caused when you take a life
And make man dependent on his wife.

For thirty years he's worked hard for you
Days out sick, no, that would never do
He has a family and mortgage to pay
Which is why he's never missed a day
He is the breadwinner after all
With head held high he can walk tall.

Now in later years with children grown
He and his wife are on their own
They settle back to enjoy life
This hardworking man and his wife.

Then quite suddenly, out of the blue
You decide, cut costs, this we must do
Our shareholders insist, increase revenue
We must make more money, what can we do?

Keep our jobs safe! I know, we'll try
Redundancies for the smaller fry.
We'll start at the bottom, the factory floor
Who needs workers, we want profits galore!

And so it came down from you on high
Redundancy for the smaller fry.
To you, just a number you've never met
After thirty years' service, good-bye, albeit.

Society grooms men to work for a living
Wife and children make them loving and giving
Work gives them a needed identity
Unemployment robs them of their dignity.

Sheila Wilmot

DO SOMETHING POSITIVE

Mother come to keep fit, my daughter cried
You'll feel much better than sitting inside
Or come to aerobics, that's really good
You'll feel the benefit, honest you would.
Have a facial, get a tint, have some new glasses,
I've noticed you squint.

You can't really enjoy just watching TV
or reading another book,
Why don't you take an interest, in the way you look?
Women of the nineties, have get up and go.
Slimming and swimming, for all in the know.
Primrose oil, and HRT you can have them all you see,
You'll feel a new woman, please believe me.

Now listen to me daughter dear,
A little word, in your shell-like ear,
I appreciate all you say to me,
But let me grow old gracefully.
I've had enough of exercise,
These are laughter lines, around my eyes.
I like my hair this shade of grey
My middle-age spread is here to stay.
So please do give your mouth a rest.
And kindly remember *mother knows best*. . .

Jacqueline Claire Davies

THE SEA

A million miles from coast to coast
She swells, and gathers life
The raging torrent of the sea
Her strength that causes strife.

The pounding of the mighty waves
That crash against the shore
The struggling of the helpless ships
As she swallows up one more.

The darkness of the deepest league
The stillness of the deep
Her wrecks, the hidden fortunes
Her secrets she will keep.

The tempest at its highest
The stillness of the ebb
She will never cease to conquer
Or be silent, like her dead.

C J Landers

NIGHT

The ticking clock, my heart at rest,
My eider down, a feathered nest,
Outside tall sentries guard the night,
And bathe the street in sodium light,
In silent, amber, artificial glow,
Cars dream of red, green, stop and go,
And as they sleep on tyred wheels,
A slinking black cat softly steals,
Yet soon comes dawn, which once again,
Divides his world of mice and men.

Neville Morgan

STATE OF THE WORLD

Just look and see, what bad deeds,
The world has done, to those who need
Who need our love, and our care,
So why is life so unfair.

They twist their little minds so much,
that childhood is lost, so out of touch
They keep the guilt hidden inside,
It hurts them so, it takes their pride

They're not the ones, that are to blame,
So give them love, not all this shame,
Help them now, while they're young,
Tell them that they've done no wrong,
They're only children, you were too
Would you like it if it happened to you

Karin Clarkson

REFLECTION

The face that you see in the mirror
is a reflection of sorrow and pain.
If you saw the chance to go forward
would you start all over again?

You sit and you study and wonder
what awaits in the future to come,
the steps that you climb to go upward,
you'll climb them just one by one.

If you trip and you fall don't go backward,
that's my word of warning to you,
just dust yourself down and keep climbing,
your courage will soon see you through.

Jeannette McShane

FRIENDSHIP

(A poem written on the occasion of an examination success and dedicated to close friends, who helped over this time)

There's a word in the English language,
A word resounding and clear,
It's a lovely word somehow - it's *'friendship'*,
And friendship is what we have here.
But how to define it, in plain simple words,
Is the task which we set ourselves now,
So let's speak our mind,
Be clear and concise,
Be brief and explain the know-how!

I'd say it's a handshake so warm and sincere,
A cheery 'hallo' or 'goodbye',
A letter with warmth in to show someone cares,
That 'something' that keeps spirits high.
A shoulder to cry on when days look quite black,
A chat with a cup of tea,
A good hearty laugh, when the rain's pouring down,
A warm word spoke twixt you and me.

A lift in the car when the bus won't arrive,
A 'yes I'll have her to tea'
Get on with the dress, and put the bulbs in,
It makes no difference to me.
She can come back at four, or play for some more,
Be bathed in the tub with the rest -
Get on with the study, you'll win in the end,
If you fight with your will and your zest.

That's friendship to me, is it like that to you?
Is it warmth, affection and cheer?
I hope it is friend, and I hope with my heart,
That you've found it in full force right here!

Brenda Bastin

GUESS WHAT

Birds flying, showers of rain,
Crystal dew - daybreak - again.
Air so fresh, the warmth of sun,
Stirs of life, the sounds of man.
Chinks of light, the depths of dark,
Cloaks of mist, the rainbow's arch.
Blooms of growth, winter's still,
Trees so proud, a natural well.
Powerful winds, angry storms,
Hail, sleet and snow,
All these we take for granted,
How little do we know.
For every breath or sign of life
That we bear witness to,
Is given, by the Grace of God especially,
For you.

Sarah E Stephenson

TO MY LOVE

When the darkness closes in,
And your walls begin to fold,
Think of those who love you,
And the compassion that they hold.

Don't be afraid to tell them,
Or reach out with your heart,
Share your fears and dreams,
When love's there you'll never part.

Don't ever think you're lonely,
When you're sitting in the dark,
Tears never break the spirit,
Of a love that's from the heart.

S Macro

TEA ON THE VICARAGE LAWN

Peeping through the hedge I see
Ladies drinking Vicarage tea,
    every afternoon
They sit on chairs with funny feet
and sip their tea from cups so neat,
    every afternoon.
They talk and laugh and eye the cakes
Arranged on pretty doilied plates,
    every afternoon
When I am quite grown up, you'll see
I'll be sipping Vicarage tea
    every afternoon
I'll sit on chairs with funny feet
And try the cakes arranged so neat,
    every afternoon
But, most of all I'll love to take
a slice of luscious chocolate cake,
    every afternoon.

Peggy Netcott

MY FRIENDS

My friends are kind, helpful and true,
And they are friendly like me and you,
they stick by me through thick and thin,
And I don't care if they're ugly or dim,
Because friends are friends right to the end,
And when I'm with them I'm not frightened,
To be myself and have some fun,
Because I know with them I will never be glum.

Joanne Thomas

MUM

In life there's often sadness
We all have our share of pain
And when we lose someone we love
Our world won't be the same.

Did I ever really thank her
For all those loving years
She shared my happiest moments
But she also shared my tears.

I'm told that time will heal my grief
As the weeks and months go by
But my love for her will never change
The memories won't die.

There's just one hope I cling to
That there is an afterlife
Where parents wait for children
And a husband finds his wife.

I hope she's now with my dear Dad
That they are together again
For me, I know that life goes on
And that sunshine follows rain.

And so it's time to say goodbye
My love to her I send
A loving Mum, a dearest Nan
But most of all my friend.

Valerie Smith

UNTITLED

Among my little treasures
There is one that I like best
One that has a memory
More precious than the rest
A little golden locket
That holds threads of Mother's hair
Yes I do remember it
Was golden and so fair
A memory that will never die
For she gave me all her care
Yes this is my treasure
One that money cannot buy
For it holds the memories
Of her life
So young to have to die.

Nancey Morgan

MY DAUGHTER

When you were born
All those years ago,
The joy I felt,
Only I will know,
Ten tiny fingers,
Ten tiny toes,
Two little cute ears,
One little button nose,
Your hair light brown,
And your eyes were blue,
You were my little girl,
And Mummy was so,
Very proud of you.

J Boote

15

WALLY'S SUITCASE

His suitcase was bright and his suitcase was large
But it still wouldn't fit on the deck of a barge
Because when he packed it Wally didn't think
And all that he left out was the old kitchen sink
In went his fishing rod and a six foot golfing brolly
Then his giant plastic cod and a massive golfing trolley
Underneath his socks and shoes were his size twelve hiking boots
A mountain of his clothes and Wally's two pet newts
It was several hours later when Wally closed his case
And set off for the airport at a breakneck pace
As he settled in his seat his case was loaded first
But halfway over London from the cargo hold it burst
There had been a mild explosion at the back of the plane
Now the contents of his suitcase fell like crazy rain
Upon the land of Epping his clobber tumbled down
To decorate the Forest and half of Epping town!

Shirley Bailey

THE TROPICAL ISLAND

It was a hot roasting day
On a tropical bay
The sun came up
And the tide ran away
Playing on the beach on your hands and knees
Feeling the weather a long long breeze
The sun came down the beach calming down
No more busy roads in the town
Coconut trees growing high in the sky
Looked in the sky saw a bird flying high.

Samantha Hodson McCoy

IGNORAMUS

I know that I am clever,
The most brilliant in the school,
I speak often to the headteacher
Because I've broken every rule.

I'm really gud at spelinng,
And know my ABD,
And I must be top dog in maths,
Teacher puts kisses for me to see.

I haven't got a real friend
And that's not really fair,
Just because I like to be first in line,
And if I'm not, I pull their hair.

I must be brighter than teacher
As she glares at me in despair,
She says she cannot keep up with me,
I said I didn't care.

My parents are so good to me
I don't have to toe the line.
They tell me to enjoy myself,
So what if I'm not at school on time.

It won't be long before I leave
And then there'll be a fuss.
They said they'll present me with a cup
Inscribed with 'Ignoramus'.

Karen Smith

MESSAGE TO A SON

When you were just a little boy
You gave me such a fright
You came in a hurry
On a wet and windy night,
The wind was howling at the door
Your mother she did moan
You had me really worried son
As I was all alone,
You had me rushing up and down the stairs
Your nappies I did bear
I really had to hurry
I was the only person there,
The water I tried hard not to spill
As up the stairs I did dash
You got me so excited
I came out in a rash,
And after It was all over
And I sat down to my tea
I realised it was my own fault
Oh silly me.

Alec G Vale

THE TORTOISE

Beneath the cabbage patch it lies
The giant tortoise with its beady eyes,
The slow reptile passes by
Carrying his shell up high.
The tortoise eats not fly nor fish
For he's looking out for a vegetarian dish.
With beak-like jaws, short tail and legs,
The friendly tortoise lays her eggs.

M Thrower

SHADOWS OF THE PAST

Oh, how I long for peace
On this little Emerald Isle
But how can we attain this
If we're fighting all the while.

Is history so important
We can't get on with life
Burn those stupid books
And end this stupid strife.

I know that I'll be criticised
They'll say 'You don't understand.
You haven't lost your husband
Or been left without a hand'.

But what about the future
If this fighting doesn't end
Are you prepared to lose your grandson
Or perhaps your very best friend.

The people of Ireland
Are known far and wide
For their wit and their humour
And showing their best side.

But when we're at home
We can't be ourselves
Not if we're reading
Those cursed books on the shelves.

So, 'burn them' I say.
In a fire red hot
Live for the future
And please, fight not.

Joan Halliday

DINKY TOYS

Dinky toys were made for boys
to push and shove all day
little cars that shone like stars
twinkled in their eyes at play
Dinky toys were made for boys
to show to their pals with pride
It gave them joy that little toy
they felt so good inside
Dinky toys were made for boys
to broom and broom with glee
a little smash a great big crash
right into an imaginary tree
Dinky toys were good to us boys
what fun we've had for years
the greatest thing a parent could bring
to erase a little boy's tears.

Stuart P Jarvis

HEAVEN'S TROUBADOUR

Listen! The skylark sings his song on high;
His notes like liquid crystals fall
Falling down to us from the sky,
And spreads his melody over us all.
Rising and falling all day long,
Scattering the Earth with effervescent song.
Hot, sleepy, tranquil peace, this summer's noon,
I couldn't wish for more.
The lark then bursts forth his joyful tune,
Becoming heaven's troubadour.

M Crossman

KINGFISHER

Kingfisher, Kingfisher
As your name suggests
When it comes to fishing
You simply are the best.
Articulate and diligent
The names of your game
There really is no other
Worthy of your name.

I glimpse your searing colours
As you flash on by
You really are quite
Beautiful to my humble eye.

Graham Dennis

LIFE

Life.
Leaving.
Living.
Looking, lamenting, loving.
Inhabiting, incorporating, inventing.
Feeding, following, finding.
Enduring, ensuring, escaping.
Developing, doing, demolishing.
Establishing, entrusting, engaging.
Adapting, adopting, adoring.
Thinking, teaching, thanking.
Holding, helping, honouring.
Departing.
Dying,
Death.

Anna

FOR SALE

Sitting thinking quietly, of many jobs to do,
Yet we cannot start one of them,
Until a sale goes through.
Four times the agents we have changed,
In only eighteen months.
Quick sales were promised every time,
But we've not completed once.
The house is too big!
The house is too small!
We cannot get the mortgage.
It's really nice, just what we want,
But sorry . . . we can't afford it!
We've dropped the price by ten thousand,
Just right for a first-time buyer.
But still we sit, as all around,
Properties sell at prices higher.
Will our new agents sell it now?
We sit with fingers crossed,
Trying not to dwell too deeply,
On the dream buys we have lost.
Perhaps this third house that we've found,
On which we've an offer accepted,
Will still be vacant when we've sold,
And we'll move in as expected.
So where's the people ready to view?
We're willing the phone to ring.
We tend to spend our weekends now,
Hopefully waiting in.

Debbie Smith

CAFÉ HAG

I go off a shopping,
To get my Coffee Hag,
I ask where it is,
I wish I hadn't, had,
No we do not sell that,
That's what they say,
So off I go, on my merry, merry way,
I find it myself,
Upon a shelf,
'Way hay',
How silly they are not knowing at all,
I go and tell them,
I found my Coffee Hag,
Oh Café Hag,
That's all they say,
What's the difference,
Anyway,
It's only coffee I say,
They don't speak like me,
I don't care anyway.

Linda Semmens

MOONRISE

I watched the tender arms of night embrace the burning sun
And softly hold that glowing gold until its fire was done.
Then from this union came the birth
That lit again the face of Earth
A wondrous birth that came so soon and claimed the sky for itself,
The moon.

B MacDonald

A SECOND CHANCE

I try to cry but tears won't come
Like the clouds that hide the sun.
My thoughts go flitting and won't stand still,
Spinning in my head like a grinding mill.
What am I, what will I be,
Lots of answers I cannot see,
My mind can't seem to make things clear
I wish I knew why I was here.

Then there you are, so good, so calm
Acting like a soothing balm
And with the light of early morn -
Bringing its promise of a sunny dawn.
I know some answers, quite a few
I know I belong, by the side of you.

A gentle love came to my mind
A love I never thought I'd find.
Life has new meaning now for me
Despair is over, now I'm free.
And like the sunshine from above
My life is filled with warmest love.

John Spencer

THE ROBIN

One day as I awoke
All to the joys of spring
Upon my little window sill
A robin there did sing
His lovely feathers so brown in colour
His lovely breast of red
So I gently closed the window
And crushed his little head.

Trevor Wright

VESTRY MEETING

There's dry rot in the belfry, damp on the vestry floor,
Tiles are off the church roof, key's lost from chapel door.
Carpet needs repairing, new candles have been bought.
Presented quite concisely, the Churchwarden's report.
Treasurer sighed in sorrow, glancing round he said,
'We must have some fund-raising, or we'll be in the red.
Parish Share goes up, while contributions fall,
Can we have some jumble sales, or tombola in the Hall?'
Secretary read out the mail received since last we met.
Sadly gave his notice in, to murmurs of regret.
Up rose Vicar to have his say, on changes he wanted made
To the form of service for Remembrance Day Parade.
A lively discussion followed, on Vicarage repairs,
Whether the Vicar needed new carpet for his stairs.
Then, 'Any other business?' Verger raised his head.
'The organ needs repairing, it's quite bad.' he said.
'With squeaks and bangs and rattles, sound comes out all wrong.
The organist gets very cross when playing at Evensong'.
Choirmaster left a note to say 'Choir will have a go
At unknown hymns and psalms, but they'd rather ones they know!
Date of next meeting noted, we got up off our chairs.
Folding hands devoutly, Vicar closed with prayers.

Wendy Morgan

PASTORAL

Sweet Suffolk maids beware!
The miracle of spring is here
It's blossom time and fields are painted gold
So long ago the shepherds by the fold
Piped their love songs by sparkling streams
And hoped to love, as in their dreams
And Cupid laughed at nature's dance
Knowing that all this beauty would enhance
Young lovers.
But now the young are so sophisticated
they are so blasé - talk of being 'dated'
Do they not know that nature has not changed?
And she has got such lovely plans arranged
Bird song - and leafy trees and scented flowers
And our young mods must yield to nature's powers
And re-enact spring's pageant once again
Sweet Suffolk maids beware!

Ethel Bestford

EARLY MORNING BIRDS

When the early morning birds do sing
I feel the joy that they do bring,
everyday they're right on time
I wish those birds could all be mine,
up with the sun those birds are free
as they fly around for all to see,
O' early morning birds I know
it breaks my heart to see you go.

I P Smyth

LOST LOVE BE ALRIGHT

My love is gone
I don't know where,
I trudge the streets
But she's not there.
I look in places where we used to go,
The clubs, the bars,
But she's not there.
I try the back streets
The down and outs,
Living in filth with meths laying around,
She took to drugs
I don't know why,
She was a lovely girl
Till the punk rock came to town,
She's changed so much
I wonder why,
But I will love her till I die.

I W Burnell

UNTITLED

I try to remember every detail,
everything you do.
The way you laugh, the way you smile,
everything about you,
the way you get embarrassed
your evil looking eyes,
your hands, your feet, and your face,
even your little lies,
the way you always look at me,
and your gentle touch,
all these things seem so small
but mean so very much.

Amanda Brown

WELCOME LITTLE ONE

So long we've waited
Now you are here
Our own little stranger
Oh, so dear

A new addition
To be protected
Given lots of attention
Never neglected

Hang the expense
You're worth every penny
Whilst never complaining
Your needs are many

Loved and sheltered
From wind and weather
There'll be sunny days
To enjoy together

You came to us
When you were two
Such grace and style
In your coat of blue

So many adventures
Still to be shared
What's round the corner?
Must be prepared

In years to come
You'll travel far
Our bright and shining
Little car.

Joan Richardson

AFTER THE MATCH

Well Terry,
At the end of the day,
The boys 'ave done well,
What more can I say -
They've given 'em 'ell.

We played the short ball,
We gave it a clout,
'Cause long and short balls
Is what football's about.

Now football, you see,
Is a game of great skill -
They kicked us a bit
And we went for the kill!

And seriously now,
All joking apart,
The boys 'ave gone out there
With gigantic 'earts

And all of them gave
One 'undred per cent
An' when the whistle was blown
It paid dividends.

Now I'm not superstitious,
Or nothing like that,
But next Wednesday's game
Is in the gods' lap.

And as for the future-
We're on the way up,
I don't believe in targets,
But we're aiming for the cup.

Steve Tribe

UNTITLED

As I look at you sleeping
I feel all those feelings
Oh so strong
That they keep me alive

You were sent to me angel
Just when I needed you
To hold, to touch, to feel.
To love me.

I won't be lonely any more
I'll kiss those days goodbye
And keep you here forever
Just you and I

I lean over to your face
And tenderly touch your skin
My breath is taken away
As you open your eyes.

Louise McCabe

JUST WAITING

It's so irritating waiting in at home.
For the plumber and the gas man.
Or the man to mend the phone
But they can't say when they'll come.
Wednesday they think.
Waiting at the airport
For the plane that's been delayed
Waiting for the postman, and waiting to be paid
But if I ever get to Heaven
I shall hear St Peter say
I'll be with you in a moment if you care to wait.

M Gouldstone

BATTLE, BEASTS, BATTLE!

'Methinks I'll have some sport today'
Tom Cat said to himself;
His long strong claws he then surveyed,
'Bulldog with these I'll pelt!'

Blackbirds, by far too small to eat,
With disdain were met;
Bobby Bulldog, King of streets,
Be ready for your fate!

Atop the fence young Tom Cat sat
With head and claws hung low;
He clawed, he scratched, he even spat
At Bobby down below.

Bobby, his pride wounded indeed,
(A cat should treat him so!)
He jumped, he growled, he even snarled
To bring that cat down low.

He jumped four feet, he jumped five feet,
Tom's tail he couldn't catch,
It swayed and swung just out of reach;
My, look how his teeth gnash!

He flexed his legs; a sturdy stance;
His body muscles bulging;
He hurled himself straight at Tom Cat -
Now in the pond they're soaking.

Penelope Dene

A PROMISE

We'll share your gladness
We, the great mountains,
We'll share the gladness that makes your heart sing.

We'll keep your secrets
We, the far valleys
We'll keep your secrets locked deep in our heart.

We'll take your weeping
We, the deep waters,
We'll take your teardrops and create a clear spring

We will protect you
And comfort and hold you,
We, the great valleys, the mountains and springs.
We will bring gladness to wrap and enfold you,
The joy and contentment that just we can bring.

Angela Cave

GETTING NOWHERE

I'm cycling through the countryside
with the sun beating on my back,
the rolling hills disappear behind
as I go along the track.

Then I'm at the seaside
with the sandy beach before me.
The seagulls fly and screech above
and the children are splashing in the sea.

The miles, they disappear with ease.
I slow the pace and stop the dream,
and I get down from my exercise bike
which is stationary in my living room!

Angela Matchett

WHAT IS A SMILE?

A smile is like the warm sun
  in summer, after a heavy shower,
A smile is like the first day of spring
  when you see a blooming flower!

A smile is like a blackbird singing,
  the buds appearing on the trees,
A smile is like a hot summer's day,
  when you feel a soft gentle breeze!

A smile is still there for all to give
  to everyone they meet,
It does not cost, it's easy to do,
  inside, or down the street.

If once a day we gave a smile,
  to all the folks we see
A lot of happiness would be spread around
  And that smile would be the key!

If a smile was used more often
  Not harsh words and rudeness an obsession,
We could all share the nice things in life,
  That smile would be the first lesson!

Stoney Broak

ONE TIME

A moment, a place, an ever lasting face,
A tick, a tock, an ever chiming clock,
A dream, a tear, an ever lasting fear,
A day, a night, an ever lasting fight,
A love, a smile, that makes it all worth while,
I hope, I pray, an ever lasting day.

Kelly Ann Green

THE BEACH

I once visited a beach house upon the
sands so golden.
This was not a place to deploy or destroy
but a place to be kept golden.
Then once I visited the beach again and to
my surprise this little beach near a town
had come to its demise.
On the beach there was rubbish and trash
all the waste of man.
Then I saw someone dumping barrels it was
a person with a dark tan.
This horrid person spotted me then turned around and ran.

Christopher Scarratt

WONDROUS FUNGUS

Mummy gets excited over leaves and plants and stuff
Of these sorts of treasures she just can't get enough
So you can imagine her delight as we walked through the woods one day
There growing out of a tree trunk as though it were modelled in clay
Was a wondrous Dryad's Saddle (we later found out the name)
What an incredible lump of fungus, she's never been quite the same.
The question was 'shall we pick it?' or leave it there to grow
The late night mob might smash it to bits and other wanderers might
never know
What a treasure was here to be found among the damp dark leaves
Only the squirrels and we have seen, or spider as her web she weaves.
'Pick it mum, go on pick it!' 'No no' protested I
'Something small might live in there, some grub or snail or fly.'
And so we left it where it was, so beauteous with its frills
and Mum returned the very next day with paints and brush and pencils!

Sue Browne

MY FRIEND AND I

I have a friend who is my mum
She's always there for everyone
I only have one thing to say
I love her more each passing day.
And when I'm sad and feeling pain
She holds my hand, and says again
'My dearest daughter, you are a dream
You know I love you, you know I'm keen,
To make you happy, and see you smile
You shouldn't cry for such a while
So cheer up girl, it's not that bad
'Cos if you don't, you'll make me sad.'

A M Lee

MY SHADOW

Wherever I go
My shadow goes too
Whatever I do
He's certain to do.
If I fish in the river,
Or climb up a tree,
I know that my shadow
Will be there with me;
If I paddle five minutes
In Willowby Pool,
If I run in to town,
If I lag towards school,
If I sit at my desk,
If I rush to my play,
My shadow will go with me
All of the way.

Ivy O Eastwick

WHAT IS A CHILD

What is a child, someone who doesn't know
The right way and the wrong way
Which is fast and which is slow.

So innocent and helpless
Someone who needs great care,
A child can feel so happy
Just knowing that you are there.

He will bring a smile back to your face,
Or make you feel quite sad,
When he's a little naughty,
Or very, very bad.

He will kiss you in the morning,
When dawn comes shining through,
And say's I love you mummy
I'll take good care of you.

He will always come home running
When he's not really sure,
It's only that he's lonely
And feeling insecure.

A child needs help and understanding
To guide them through their life
To help them through the milestones
through trouble and strife.

If you have the wonderful gift of children
You will understand I'm sure
God gave us little children,
To love and to adore.

Jean Skates

OH I MISS YOU

Since the night I walked away
my life has been sad and blue
while you were on holiday
I really did miss you
the days have been so long
and I've been lonesome and blue
looking at your photographs
as they remind me of you

I think of you when I'm asleep
in bed I'm all lone
the tears run down my cheek
and I feel run down
I know the days will soon fly
and you will be back with me
the suffering I'm feeling now
will no longer be

Each minute became an hour
and each hour was so slow
but I really do love you
I know that you know
absence makes the heart grow fonder
that's what people say
I'll be looking out for you
when you come home on Monday

A S Clarke

ODE TO THE WEEKEND

Oh, the joy of weekday Friday
And the rest from toil and gloom
With the prospects of the weekend
Saturday won't come too soon.

Wake up early Saturday morning.
Load the car with packs and boots
Forgetting now the smart appearance
Away with tie and well-pressed suits.

Park the car and lace the boots up
check the map and off we go.
Up the ridge and to the summit
See the fields stretched out below.

Just to linger on the hill tops
Never mind the wind and rain
In the company of a loved one
Freedom from the rat race train

Sitting huddled 'neath a great rock
Eating sandwiches and pie
Hot refreshment from the thermos
Food and drink which satisfy.

Down the valley we return now
Wind and rain are getting worse
Never, mind, though, we are happy
Freed from all the weekday curse.

Now it's Sunday we're relaxing
Time to think and be inspired
Resting talking dozing gently
Of all the days - the one admired

Monday morning - back to work now
Not too bad this toil and strain
Weekend memories give us courage
To accept the rat race train.

G S Waterfield

INSOMNIAC

What a way to spend a sleepless night
Staring at the curtains and looking at the light

Listening to every noise and hearing every creek
Your eyes feeling heavy but still you can't sleep

Hearing strange voices seeing shadows on the wall
Listening to creaking doors and footsteps in the hall

Should you get up and forget about your pillow
Or should you lay still and hope for some sleep tomorrow

Tossing and turning, the bed clothes in a heap
Your eyes feel like lead, but still you can't sleep

Should you have a hot drink? Chocolate or something like that
If you don't get some sleep soon, you'll feel like a bat

You start to hear birds singing and watch the dawn break
Still you can't believe it, but you're still wide awake

You've been awake all night, just laid and looked about
There's people getting up, there's people starting to shout

Time to get up and get dressed, it's enough to make you weep
You know when you've had breakfast, you'll drop off to sleep.

Roy Hunter

BENJY

His eyes are soft and velvet brown,
And the light shines out of there,
An expression so kind,
With inquisitive mind,
'Neath a tuft of downy hair,
So sharp, so quick and ready,
A shadow forever there,
With a constant true devotion,
And a heart so full of care,
And through life's disappointments,
And every time I cried,
On him I could depend
To be there at my side,
And for his love, his loyalty,
I thank God with a prayer,
For I know that such devotion
In humanity, is rare . . .

Barbara Huffey

THE DAFFODILS

One morning as I was drawing,
Near the river blue,
I saw some daffodils swaying to and fro.
As soon as I saw them they looked like the sun,
Tall yellow soldiers blowing their trumpets.
They were medium size and they looked like
they were talking to each other;
I started to draw them when . . .
The rain came, drip, drop, drip, drop, never mind.
But in a few minutes the sun shined!

Katy Kettleborough

1994

'Twas in 1994
That a knock came at the door
And on the step there stood a man
I'd never seen before.

'You don't know me,' said he.
(Which is true, as you can see;
For I'd never ever met him
As I mentioned formerly).

He raised his hat and bowed
And he said, not very loud,
'I don't know you, either.'
Then he vanished in the crowd.

B G Simons

WAR

War is here in my land.
I just want to bury my
head in the sand.

Bombs, guns, a person is dying.
Everyone in the village is crying.
Men women children too
help us soon, please do.

My friend has died, ten she was.
What a very tragic loss.
Now my house is to the floor.
My clothes my shoes, are no more.
I just want peace in my land,
I really hope you understand.

Sophie Louise Moore

A WISH

I would like to be an artist
With all the skill that that implies
Of lovely things would make a list
And at the break of day arise

I would paint for all to see
Amid its hallowed acres there
The old church at Drumcree
Standing so stately and fair

To capture the lovely butterfly
Emerging from its chrysalis.
Soaring up towards the sky
Rejoicing in its new-found bliss.

Is it too much to ask:-
How to capture the morning dew
And catch the spider at her task
A secret that I wish I knew.

To paint the glowing rainbow
After the springtime rain
Shining forth that we might know
God's promises are not in vain.

When the day's tasks are done
On an evening calm and still
I would paint the sinking sun
From the bridge at Blennerville.

Wondrous gifts from Heaven
To show the beauty of the earth
To the artist truly given
Is a gift of priceless worth.

Maureen Hawthorne

DESTINED TO FLY

Out on the summer azure sky,
My knight of feathers aims up high,
Caressing the white virgin cloud,
Head held mighty, breast thrust proud.

He swoops and skates on air's own ice,
Looping once, to tempt and entice
Earth's sweet green blanket beneath,
Dappled with lingering purple heath.

The scent of heaven, close to feel
The breath of purity, a life unreal,
A warmth of the sun begs him to sing,
A bullet whispers through his wing.

Beads of blood, blue splashed red,
Tranquillity shattered, his body dead,
Life's spirit lives, and soars still high
My knight of feathers, destined to die.

Janice Moore

LONELY

I am sat in a cold, dark, run-down deserted house.
Doesn't anyone care?
I'm alone at night, only the company of rats and mice around me.
Doesn't anyone care?
Scraps from dustbins along the streets - that's my daily ration.
Doesn't anyone care?
The odd drop in a coke can left in the street - that's all the drink I get.
Doesn't anyone care?
Boxes without blankets - that's all I ever have for rest.
Doesn't anyone in the world care?

Claire Hartell (11)

UNTITLED

There was a fellow
Up our street
They called him Smoky Joe
He used to sit on the village seat
With his girlfriend he called Flo.
They'd sit there puffin' their cares away
All covered in nicotine
Puffin' puffin' puffin' all day.
Ooh blimey what a scene.
then one day the bulldozer came
And said I'm sorry Joe
It is such a crying shame
Your seat has got to go
Said Joe to Flo, I think that it
Is time that we were wed
Instead of sitting
On the village seat
We could go home to bed
We were going out to tea
Have you some dumplins Nan
I have no suet you can see
So up the shop they ran.

Mildred

GOLDEN VALUES

Come and see the sunset all red and bright and gay,
Not tonight I beg you I've had such a busy day,
The roses red they fill the air with perfume that is all too rare,
They are in the garden for you to see, sorry I'm just watching TV,

A full moon shines from high above, it lights the earth it's bright and good,
But I am busily engaged I'm playing cards, it's as it should,
The bubbling brook cascades along it sounds of music and of song,
My present thoughts say just one thing to get a drink give the bell a ring,
The stars they twinkle in the sky like diamonds up so very high,
The diamonds I like best to see, are those down here that belong to me.

The bumble bee is busy, the sky is blue above,
The earth gives forth its goodness to move me I need a shove,
I really am not happy with cards TV and toys,
I'm bored with drinks and diamonds and bills I can't afford,

My pockets are almost empty I'm full of joy and good,
I've watched the lambs a'skipping in the meadow by the wood,
At last I've seen that peace of mind can not be bought with money
The joys of simple pleasures are there for all in ample measure.

Jack Meadows

COLIN'S LATEST PROJECT

The Enfield bike came in boxes
For Colin to build
He set about the task
He was absolutely thrilled
It took a few months
He did a good job
He also made a profit
In fact we both made a few bob.

Brenda Ashworth

HEATHER

Heather shining on the hillside,
       on a rainy day,
Flowers shake off the raindrops
       in a misty spray.

Heather sparkling on the hillside,
       in a winter snow,
Making fairy patterns
       in the bright, bright snow.

Purple heather bright in sunlight
In a scented air; with sweet nectar,
Bees are busy there.

Winifred Linnett

MEDITATIONS OF THE SEA

I love to wander by the shore
And listen to the sea.
As it gently bathes its golden floor,
And washes down the scree.
Its silver band like diamonds rare
All shimmering in the sun,
Gives kisses to the pebbles there
And links of beauty spun.
And as I listen to each sound
Sweet music is unfolding.
I watch the white topped waves abound
With robes of colour beholding.
And as I stroll and view these sights
To nature I am owing.
To witness one of her delights,
With its grace and beauty showing.

Edith M Smith

QUIET LIFE

The sun is shining through the trees
Birds are singing in the breeze
Rabbits playing in the fields
Farmers reaping in their yield.

Cows are mooing as they stand
On this lovely pastured land
Sheep are baaing loud and clear
Now I see some wild deer.

The countryside means much to me
As I capture the scenery
Horses roaming all around
Sights like these not seen in town.

Country folk are full of fun
Into town they never come
Tractors trailers carts they own
Through the country they do roam.

Heading back across the dale
Townsfolk people I can tell
What a life these people lead
Living off the land they feed.

D Ford

HOW ROMANTIC

I like to walk right by your side,
and hold hands along the road,
you stop to kiss me lovingly,
then whisper that you love me loads.

When we're out for an evening together,
in a really crowded place,
you're right by my side all evening,
not to let anyone invade our space.

Sometimes you like to surprise me,
and you'll take me out to dine,
we'll laugh and talk for ages,
as we share a bottle of wine.

As the evening draws to an end,
and when we walk, I hold your arm,
you guide me through the darkest night,
and always protect me, from any harm.

When we arrive home you'll hang my coat,
the shoes you remove from my feet,
all evening you've been such a gentleman,
and you've treated me, so very sweet.

Last of all we'll settle in bed,
where it's so warm and very snug,
you'll hold me in your arms all night,
and give me a wonderful hug.

Karen Squire

THE COAST - NORFOLK

Beyond the creek,
Out on the bar,
That rides above the tide,
The waders stand, in line at rest
One legged, braced against the breeze
Like figures on some ancient frieze.

While o'er the pools
Within the marsh,
Where samphire pickers go
Stark white against the azure blue,
The gulls do rise, fall back, and rise
Like drifts of flurried snow

E Leahy

THE ROAD TO SNOWSHILL

The Snowshill road from Broadway
Runs straight to the top of the hill,
With hillside views on either side
And a stream running down to a mill.

The Snowshill road was a carefree road
Which we travelled as choirboys with glee,
To play cricket against the Snowshill boys
With a short break at Milyaik's for tea.

The Snowshill road was a friendly road
As it led to old schoolmates I knew,
The Hodges', the Turner's, the Diston's.
Good friends and good cricketers too.

Reginal E Stokes

FRIENDS

The garden birds who come to feed
upon the crumbs and nuts and seed
or have a drink from bowl or bath
which we have on the garden path.

Pigeons feed at early morn
but on greens and shoots new born
Sparrows always on the go
seem to flutter to and fro.

The Blackbird with his yellow bill
Chaffinch on the window sill
And Robin foraging around
for bugs and grubs upon the ground.

The Starlings always seem to squabble
until the Jackdaws come and hobble
stealing all the food in sight
and putting other birds to flight.

The little Wren stays close to ground
keeping out of sight and sound
while Blue Tits flit like little clowns
tumbling, spinning, upside down.

As I watch them feed and drink
or splashing in the bath - I think
it's wonderful to see them all
watch them fly, hear them call.

J Kincaid

THE FAMOUS FIVE

There were five bright blokes in an army camp
Naught on earth their spirits would damp.
There was Jim and Bob, Charlie and Ron
And last of all that terrible John.
Now Jim was a lad from Hendon way.
There once on a time he earned his pay.
Bob from Durham used paper and paint
A comical bloke with a smile quite quaint
Charlie hails from London city
And cooks the grub more's the pity.
Ron's a Yorkie and that says enough
His life with the rest is rather rough
Johnny's a lad from Huddersfield town.
With divvy and Co-op cheques he's weighted down.
These five scrounged on through light and dark
Always ready for fun and a lark
But luck was out and so they parted.
Good friendship ne'er stops once it's started.
May fate be kind and God be good.
To keep this friendship as it stood.
And when this strife has passed away
We hope to meet one peaceful day.
And there once more in civvy's at last
We'll yarn again of good times past.

R Moxon

LOVE'S LAST CALL

One dark winter's night as I sat down to write.
I felt a cold presence in the dim candle light.
I gazed at the door as my true love walked in,
Whispering darling my darling please leave down your pen.

For I have your love letter five minutes read,
Before you had started I was already dead.
I just died this evening, my parents don't know
And I must go and see them before the cock's crow.
But I'll be with you till you meet with me,
In a wonderful Heaven far from purgatory.

My hand was now shaking, my heart it did ache
As I wondered what action or steps I should take.
Was this just a nightmare and would it go away,
With the rise of the sun and the start of the day.
No this was sad reality, dear life had passed her by,
My love had called on me to say her last goodbye.

Is eternity a life time, a minute or an hour,
Is a tiny seed the ending or the starting of a flower.

Bernard Reilly

HOPE?

You have a new love now of enviable grace,
You loved me once, I bore your child,
But could not match your pace
Your boundless energy,
So, in the end I had to set you free.
Think of me sometimes in the still small hours,
When arms entwined, you'd whisper words of love and kiss me.
Remember please my love, oh please
And just a little - miss me.

N Goodill

MY DREAM

I would like to fly into the sky
And through the clouds which are so high
They look so soft and fluffy to touch
It is only a dream, I dream so much
My dream one day nearly came true
As off to Portugal I flew
We flew so high up in the sky
The clouds that I dream about, passing by
The clouds alas, I couldn't touch
So it still remains my dream
Because I dream so much.

Thelma Hill

THE FOUR SEASONS

Trees are awake, for spring is here
Daffodils bloom with heads in the air,
Birds singing gaily and full of zest
Seeking a hide away to build a nest.

Summer again with blue skies above
Holiday season the time we all love
Buckets and spades a nice stretch of sand
Relax in the sun makes life so grand.

Autumn is here and all the flowers fade
Trees shed their leaves of a beautiful shade
Days are shorter and cooler at night
Colourful season a wonderful sight.

Cold winter winds and snow everywhere
Frozen lakes and birds in despair
We have to accept there must be a reason
Should any such change take place in a season.

Doreen Buhlemann

DESERT SONG FOR A CAMEL

Bones bleached, brittle, blanched a brilliant white,
      Peep through the orange haze of morn's first light;
Embedded there in sand - no winding sheet;
      Laid bare to eastern sun's relentless heat.

The hump-shape still intact, the skull with empty eyes,
      Indecently exposed he lies - a landing-strip for flies;
A shipwreck on a barren stretch of land;
      His final port, a lonely bank of sand.

With last few strides, as after food he sought,
      I wonder did he entertain the thought,
That somehow after death he'd come alive again;
      Before his stumbling knees jack-knifed him to oblivion.

What life would he resume? What status would he seek?
      Perhaps a King - a Prince - or oil-rich Arab Sheikh.

Joe McGrory

OUT MY WINDOW

I sit and watch through plated glass
And see the world fly past the grass
The lovely sights that to be seen
Just fade away like they've never been
The sky is blue
And grass so green . . .
I like the place
And feel I cannot go
But the world goes fast and not so slow
Now I must leave this window frame
And return to sadness from where I came

Anita Gallacher

DEDICATED TO KELLY

She lies down the garden
In a special spot tendered by me

I often sit and think
Of the happy times we had together
With her sitting on my knee

The first time I saw her
I fell for her right away
I had already made up my mind
She would be mine one day

She could never get on with Bodie
They used to fight and they could never agree
But her little friend Drummer were inseparable
you see

I made up my mind to buy her
With no luck at all
I thought I would have no trouble
As she was going to be very small

Then one day I received a phone call
To tell me she was mine
So everything I had hoped for turned out fine

The day came for her to say goodbye
She went to her box in the corner
To lay down and die
I stopped with her to the end
Holding the paw of my little friend.

J Bateman

REMEMBRANCE

Another month another year
When will this war be ended
The land and seas we love so dear
Just had to be defended

Men and youths fought side by side
Some returned but others died
Women worked from morn till night
To keep the home fires burning bright

Our soldiers marched
In all conditions
Never knowing ever hoping
The word would come
'They have surrendered'
Would they hear it
They all wondered

The Army the Navy
The Air Force too
Deserve our thanks and gratitude
If not for them
This land would be
A brotherland of Germany

J Brennan

STILL BEGGING

These days are no better
In fact these days are worse
They're just as bad as when Charles Dickens walked the earth
Begging on the corners for a crust of bread
Begging for a room to rest thee weary head
No-one wants to know
No-one wants to care
As long as they have everything
Why should they have to share.

Brenda Walton

MANY KINDS OF LOVE

There are many different kinds of love,
Which we transmit, to each other,
There is the love we feel for our parents,
There's the bonding of sister and brother.

With friends who we are fond of
And family loyalty we are true to,
There's the love we feel for a hero,
A warm glow in awe, of something new.

A mother's love for her offspring
The joy that closeness brings,
Raptures of a contented wife
Jealous love is a dangerous thing.

Our natural desire, from early years
Is to be loved, by everyone.
We all enjoy this special privilege
To shower our love upon.

Joan Hubbard

MY BUNDLE OF JOY

I was feeling down,
I was feeling low,
As from my job I had to go
The future looked dull,
The future looked dim,
All I could do was bear it and grin.

Then one day through all my pain and strife,
A little puppy bounced into my life
He sits upon my lap, or lays beside my feet
A smack when naughty when good a treat.

'Benji' I called, and in he came,
As if to say 'yes that's my name'
We play, we run and have great fun.

I no longer feel down,
I no longer feel low,
And it's all due to that little so and so.

But he is so full of love, obedient, and wise,
My heart just melts with one look,
From those spaniel eyes.

J Strong

SPRING

New born lambs grazing
Daffodils sprout during the Maying
Oh what fun I have in spring
I just enjoy to dance and sing
We put the clocks an hour ahead
And so you don't get as long in bed.

Erin Lothian (9)

MY NANNY

My nanny's a witch, she is you know, she is.
I saw her switch off her telly, just by snapping her fingers,
She gives me lovely dinner,
Witches dinner, it is you know, it is.

My grandad asked her to make him some chewing gum,
So she rubbed her hands together, and then she blew in them,
And made him half a packet.
She did you know, she did.

My nanny's got an invisible cat,
She has, you know, she has,
When my grandad went to stroke it, he got his hand all scratched,
He did, you know, he did.

My nanny's a witch, she is you know, she is.
My grandad, told me!

Patrick D Harte

AN ANGLER'S DREAM

At the end of the day I go to bed
and lay down my weary head.
I dream of the big fish
that got away and lived
to fight another day.
I dream of the next time I fish in the lake
of a place that I know is the best.
I dream of the big fish that will take my bait
And hope I don't strike too soon or too late.
I dream when my line is tight that I will strike just right.
I dream the big fish that I have on
will give me my best fight.

William Orr

UNTITLED

In 1904 as a young lad,
yes you've guessed I was my dad
The honest truths, no lie
A Scottish regiment the HLI
In 1907 to India did go
World War 1914 to fight the foe
In the trench and left for dead
shrapnel bleeding wound in his head
Taken POW by the Germans
5 years underfed suffering by their hands
5 children lost our mother in schooldays
Dad had to be both in many ways
He prayed a lot it was in vain
For he suffered lots of pain
His many grandchildren did not see
He never reach age as OAP
ARP in World War Two as well
Now this country gone to hell
Looking down you see sign
Form sign form sign
It's free country they used to say

Them that said it have passed away
Signing forms and charity is a must
European folks better off than us
With plenty of things and food on the table
Us British Council Tax Rate now if able
The gas electric water insurance mortgage TV.
Us pensioners get nothing free
A hearing aid meal on wheels
Us proud British great deal
Cousins in families went far away
Australia Canada and the USA

Forty years and good job too
Only one form to sign true
I wonder why sometimes I didn't go
The state I am in you never know
£10 it cost to go by boat
pavement victim now I gloat

Scotch Tommy

DRINK YOU AND ME

O come and drink with me
Beside that sea
And you and he will be
Forever free
Tarry and you and me will never be

Tis time you came away with me
Oh folly me
Take time with you and me
I come alive near that sea
Perhaps drink in my body awaketh me
Will you forever be with me.

Sit in lovely Cambridge fields
See bees fly
Think I don't know why
Peace of night comes at last
You're in my dreams and I think of thee
Will you never be with me?

Oh come along and take to my side
Listen to whispering trees
As twins and me pass you see
Sitting with lovely meadow, with buttercups array
The sun has come to bring a new day.

K Latham

OUR VILLAGE SHOP

At our local village shop, in the Cotswold hills,
Away from crowds and bustle, and the rows of checkout tills,
Where one can stop and have a chat, with friends that come and buy,
So many goods they have displayed, like bacon meat and pies,
Vege's, tins, and biscuits, paper hankies too,
Birthday cards along a shelf, so many to browse through,
Daily papers are there too, for us to keep in touch,
Fancy cakes and goodies, that tempt us all too much,
But personal service is the thing, the smile the nod the wink,
That little bit of extra time, for us to stop and think,
The friendly smile the little joke, help to make the day,
Pay the bill and pack your bag, go happy on your way,
Tomorrow is another day, so hope will never cease,
To be the centre meeting place, where we can shop in peace.

M Scrivens

OH WHAT A GROOVER

Denim jeans with holes in, faded to a paler blue,
Heavy soled boots scuffed so as not to look brand new,
Rings on all the fingers like knuckle dusters were,
She really does look a mess, just take a look at her,
Cheese-cloth shirts and hippy gear surely will astound,
Burning incense oil and josssticks she will soon pass around,
Pink Floyd and Led Zeppelin blaring out with a loud boom,
Head-banging in the kitchen and also the front room,
Yes she's really gone now totally in a world of her own,
And all I can do about is have a real old moan,
Why don't you grow up, act your age this I would appreciate,
You're not a kid anymore but my mum of thirty-eight.

Julie Block

LEARNERS' DILEMMA

In a circle, ringers stand,
Bell ropes ready, in their hands.
Tail trapped, between the thumb,
Sally clasped, this should be fun.

Treble shouts! Look too, she's gone,
Bells ring out their cheerful song.
When rounds are struck, and sound OK,
Plain Hunt is called, to some dismay.

Bells are striking, all in place,
The Hunt is rung, it's quite a chase.
Ropes and Sallys, up and down,
Ringers cast their eyes around.

Second bell, begins to falter,
Order of the bells now alter.
As the bells begin to clash,
A shout goes out, rounds! 'At last'.

A ringer knows to keep his place,
To clash with bells, is a disgrace.
Red faced and flushed, a bell's pulled in,
Just in time, the rounds begin.

Ivan Langham

GNOME

Never alone in the garden we stand
Short fat and dumpy with colours so grand
All different shapes and sizes we come
Painting our scene in the glorious sun
Strange and mysteriously move though we might
You will never be sure of this spectacular sight
Some say were magic casting our spells
Whether were fishing or guarding the wells
A wonderful sight whether many or few
We gleam our attire in the early morning dew
Sincere is our friendship in the birds and the bees
And deep our respect for the flowers and trees
Always with a smile and never a frown
My coat of many colours just like a clown
But a gnome will be sad if he is not in his place
You will know at a glance by the look on his face
So if you see a gnome stripped of his glory
Give him a home and he will paint you a story

Gary Paul Clarke

THE NIGHT

The night,
It is so special and alight.
All the things for me to see,
Cars and buses and vans.
Stars that twinkle in turn
The houses that stand so still and stern,
And in the day
They come alive and gay
There's so much to see at night,
It is so special and alight.

Katie Brewer (5)

SOMEWHERE I PLANTED A WISH ...

Somewhere I planted a wish and it grew into a tree, tall and strong.
Its leaves were green and shiny and I shed tears on it to make it grow.
The more tears that I shed the stronger it became until one day it matured.
As time went by it grew older but the wind, storms and snow
enhanced its beauty and nothing could stop me from admiring it
fascinated by its splendour and height.
People began to notice my tree and they,
instead of admiring it began to hurt it.
They carved names on its trunk hung ropes from his boughs, pulled branches
from his roots.
I cried with pity when I saw what they had done to him.
So I built a high fence all around him.
In time he healed from his wounds
but the names were still carved in his trunk.
How could they do this to you I cried, my heart bleeding.
But even as I look upon you, disfigured for life,
I still feel the love within my heart
that I felt for you when I made that wish.
Then one day I turned to look at you and you were gone.
I looked up and saw that you had been transformed into a star.
You shone brighter than any other. You lit my way.
No-one can hurt you now you are safe.
I can look up to you, you are very special because
I wished upon you, my star, and that wish came true.

Diane Kalaher

THE DEATH OF NELLY MOSER
(Dedicated to Ian, Phillis and May)

Who really murdered Nelly Moser?
        That my friend is quite a poser.
Was it Ian who left around
        Near her roots, upon the ground.
A pressure gun full of spray
        Temptingly ready for use that day?
Or was it May who with gardener's eye
        Spotted a profusion of green fly?
May was never one to shirk
        With the 'insecticide' went to work.
Soon the spray began to flow
        On Nelly's leaves, above below.
But my friends so sad to say,
        Nelly Moser died that day.
Yes! Nelly's dead, knocked on the head,
        It was a herbicide instead.

J K Wilkinson

UNTITLED

Dear Lord give me strength to live
All my love to you I will give
You make my life so worthwhile
When I am down you make me smile
When I think I can't go on
There is faith when I had none
On the cross for me you died
And you'll always be by my side
All my life I'll spend with you
Because no other is so true.

Lynn Duke

VISITORS

We love people to visit, night or day
And they are always welcome to stay.
Usually it's only my husband and me
Sitting watching TV
So if anyone comes round
It goes off - not a sound!

We ask about each other's health
(It isn't done to talk about wealth)
And generally chat of this and that
Maybe about the dog or the cat,
I ask if anyone would like coffee or tea?
Whatever - It's no bother to me.

Our faces were happy and glowing
Then our visitors said they must be going.
Now they have departed
It's so quiet, we're downhearted
The washing up is done after the tea
So suppose it's now back to the TV.

Joan Vincent

A LIFE'S EXISTENCE

Do you wonder what the future may hold,
does it hold one for you and me,
we never know, for it remains untold,
like a deep rooted family tree.

We do not know, the future or past,
or how long we're here to stay,
life is a visit, we're not born to last,
be happy for each living day.

Julie Winter

TEARFUL EYE

A tearful glance moved to the right
And shone the crystal leaves,
That lay so light and delicate
Upon the ghostly trees.

The silver stems of sparkling grass
Gave bright this tearful eye,
Their fluffy heads of tiny stars
Disguised the winter rye.

A tear drop fell to freeze on ice
A glistening frozen stream,
That seemed to change with winter moon
Which gave a sharp bright beam.

The stones seemed glass to tearful eye
So pure and white with frost,
So soft and smooth and precious now
With all their darkness lost.

The moss lay flat as ancient lace
So stiff and fragile lay,
That tearful eye put out his hand
To feel its webby spray.

The frost had come and snow would fall
And tearful eye would go,
For tearful eye was pure born rain
That soon would freeze with snow.

J Byrne

JEWELS OF AUTUMN

Whilst walking through a woodland glade
Some of God's gifts I found displayed
Swirling, twirling to the ground
Shades of gold, red, rust and brown.
Sunlight filtering through the trees
Young and old scuffing, crispy leaves.
A colourful carpet all around
Jewels, from mother nature's crown,
Globules of sparkling, glistening dew.
Bring forth colours of brightest hue.
Insects scampering here and there
Their winter homes to prepare.
Stately pines of darkest green
Adorn this jewelled, autumn scene.
Looking up through branches bare
I see wispy clouds, scudding through the air
The mellow sun behind these hide.
Then bursts forth, with warmth and pride,
To shine and gaze on mother earth
A colourful world to which God gave birth.

Ruth James

PARTNERS

When we were married they told us we were one -
But they never told us what to do when half a one was gone
What to do with half a life or half a will to care?
What do you do with half a heart now the other half's not there?
You were the other half of me a heart linked to my own
What do I do, with half a life now I am on my own?

R Reay

LIVING IN HOPE

I haven't won the lottery,
Each week I pay my pound.
I check my ticket when the balls roll out,
But my numbers are never found.

I often dream of what I'd do,
If the millions I did win.
I would make a lot of people happy,
I'd look after kith and kin.

I would tell my boss to stick his job,
I would travel far and wide.
And live a life of luxury,
I'd do things I've never tried.

I'll keep on trying and having a go
Who knows? One day I'll win.
But I suppose I'll have to keep going to work,
Until my ship comes in.

Brian Kimberlin

A COLD WINTER'S DAY

The bitter air, and watery sky,
Frost bitten trees, they moan nearby,
The icy ponds, and frozen streams,
Their once warm waters, make chilly screams,
The snow covered, hills, and fields, and greens,
Their once lust textures, cannot be seen,
Enhanced with snow, and ice, and frost,
Their well known features, look almost lost,
The hot warm sun, seems far away,
It certainly is, a cold winter's day.

Christopher Evans

THE CALL OF SILENCE

I who made the sky that gleams with the glory of the sun,
I who caused the young foal to rise upon his legs and run,
I who made the laughter and the tears that flow from every heart,
I who gave you comfort when every other comfort did depart,

I who gave the breath of life to every living thing,
I who inspires every new dawn bird to sing,
I who planted every seed that brings bread from the soil,
I who labour with you and share in all your daily toil,

I am there when you stumble to pick up your soul,
I am the one who makes the blind and the cripple whole,
I am he who takes you on when your spirit begins to fail,
I am he who gives grace to the humble the meek and the frail,

I it is who fight for the oppressed the enslaved the Satan bound,
I who break the chains and cast them to the ground,
I am he who sends the silver rain from the summer sky,
I who gives you truth when the world sells you a lie,

I who am the sunbeam that makes the river gleam,
I who gives you rest by every peaceful stream,
I who am the voice in all your children's laughter,
I am the strength of your faith and the blessings that come after.

I am that rock of hope when your heart is backsliding,
I am your salvation the safe place for you to hide in,
I am that mercy and truth that you find in my grace,
I am he who runs with you in life's traumatic race,

I who shines in the moon's face and illuminate the stars,
I who am the mighty healer who heals your inner scars,
I am the buds of spring the green leaves of every wood,
I am the life of earth the spirit soul and blood.

P F Dews

GOD'S WORLD

God gave us the flowers, that bloom in the spring,
And the tiny birds, that whistle and sing,
He gave us the sunshine, a rainbow and showers,
A wonderful world, made by God's mighty power.

He gave us the mountains, the rivers and streams,
And woodlands and valleys that look so serene,
He gave man the knowledge, to write music and hymns,
So when we all gather, can sing praises to him.

He gave us the seas and a moon that shines light,
That shows us the way, when we walk out at night,
He gave us each other to love and to cherish,
Gave us his promise, that none will ere' perish.

A world that is bounteous, enough for us all,
Is being spoiled by man, whose greed ruins all,
A world full of beauty, so wondrous and bright,
Is slowly becoming a world full of plight.

This beautiful world which God gave to us,
Needs care and attention, not abuse and distrust,
So just make the time to sit and reflect,
Each things God created that turned out perfect.

Jean

SYMPHONY

Magical, mystical music, floating on the air,
Floating, upward, upward, like a spiral stair
Carried on a summer breeze,
Onward o'er the hill.
Fading, softly, softly, then all again is still.
What was the symphony I heard?
Was it all a dream?
No, twas the symphony of nature,
Of birds and trickling stream.
Close your eyes and listen, it's here all around you
The concerto of the falling leaves,
The dripping of morning dew.
The bubbling of water, trickling over stone.
The sighing of the evening wind,
Through grass before it's mown.
In the croaking of the bullfrog,
The humming of the bee.
Nature's orchestra performing
Its musical fantasy.

Theresa Miles

THE SPEECH

Ladies and gentlemen,
Lords and tramps,
Giant gorillas and killer ants,
Enormous beetles and pussy cats,
Birds and dogs and don't forget bats,
Tiny elephants and massive bees,
Huge mice and square fleas,
Baby tigers and cute snow deer,
Raise a glass of beer,
to Mr and Mrs Leech as they prepare to
make a speech.

Kevin Thorpe

ODE TO MY COATHANGERS

I have some coathangers - in fact, I have many,
But why? I have never bought any.
Where do they come from? Where do they go?
I don't know.

I moved flat and packed all my stuff.
Everything in boxes even the fluff!
I didn't take my coathangers, I simply forgot,
But apart from them, I packed the lot.

When I arrived at my new address;
I began to unpack. What a mess!
I started to organise my clothes,
Colour co-ordinated in tidy rows.
But when I opened the wardrobe door,
Oh! I've never had such a shock before.
Before my eyes, what could I see?
My coathangers had arrived before me!

Elaine Malcolmson

ME AND MY DOG

I take my dog for a walk everyday
And when we get to the park we like to play.

On the field we run around,
Making quite a lot of sound.

I throw the ball for her to bring
She chases after it like a spring

She runs back tail wagging clutching the ball
Standing proud and straight and tall

When we get home after our tiring day
In front of the fire we like to lay.

Kirsty Dawson

CLIFTON SUSPENSION BRIDGE

High above the Avon Gorge the bridge at Clifton stands.
This is Brunel's masterpiece, Majestic, Regal, Grand.
It stands for everyone to see,
Part of Bristol's history,
And all who see it will agree,
None finer in the land.

At Hungerford a Brunel bridge once spanned from shore to shore
Through progress and the Railway train, alas it is no more.
There, Charing Cross was built to stay,
The chains to Bristol found their way,
They've done their work from day to day
Since 1864.

Isambard Kingdom Brunel, Engineer by deed and mind.
Designed this great suspension bridge, then died in '59
And so, in memory of their friend,
Hawkshaw, Barlow and their men,
Brought the work to a happy end.
Now shared by all mankind.

Tony Fuller

THE JOY OF SPRING

In spring the birds start to sing
Cause winter's gone the cold old thing.
The children all come out to play
When they see a sunny day.
Spring it comes round once a year
do you remember last time it was here.
Children laughing while they play
in the grass and in the hay.
Spring is nice spring is fine
Spring is such a happy time.

Caroline Johnston

BABY

This is the birth of a human being
Daylight for the first time seeing
Laid in the midwife's arms.
Dad waiting with outstretched palms
To hold tenderly this new life
Lovingly pass this child to his wife
Mother holds her baby with care.
Gently stroking its soft brown hair
Baby lays on his mother to rest
Coaxing him onto a full warm breast
Gently touches his chin to tilt.
His first experience of mother's milk
Now mum and baby get sleep they need
The miracle of life from a tiny seed
In a cot with soft warm covers.
This perfect baby conceived by lovers.

Margaret Sanders

EASTER TIME

Easter time will soon come around
When we are out in the garden, looking for eggs to be found
We know they are hidden, amongst the shrubs and flowers
And it could take us all, quite a few hours.

The first one to find, an egg shouts for joy
Whether it be, a girl or a boy
We all get excited, and have a great day
Then later on, we go down, to the church to pray.

We pray at Easter time, for the Lord above
Who came down from Heaven, to give us his love
Love and trust in the Lord said He
Then after all the singing, it was home for tea.

Elizabeth Ann Collis

THE FACE OF LIFE

The face is made of just three things,
>   The eyes, the nose, and a mouth that sings,
With lips that we all use to kiss,
>   To help one live a life of bliss.

The lips we use to take the food,
>   To keep one fit and in the mood,
To live your life the best you can,
>   Not just to be a wonder man.

Now life depends upon those lips,
>   There's more to them that eating chips,
They hold a thing some call a 'fagg'
>   The smoke from these could make one 'sagg'

Your mouth feels if you've eaten grit,
>   In time you'll start to cough and spit,
It's then you'll wish the cigs in hell,
>   Because of them you don't feel well.

In time your breath will heave and sigh,
>   You'll think about the years gone by,
When you could run and jump with ease,
>   But now you 'sagg' upon your knees.

Your friends at work may even say,
>   You smell like smoke so go away,
The only way to stop this stink,
>   Is throw the cigs all down the sink.

To all of you when reading this,
>   Make sure you have a life of bliss,
Don't buy the things that cause ill health,
>   The money saved increases wealth.

Gerald Marsh

I KNEW SOME KIDS ONCE

When we were kids we used to make trolleys
And zoom off down the street
In the beginning they hadn't got no brakes
So we just used to use our feet

We used some planks and old pram wheels
Bent nails and rope as well
But some trolleys had got customised
With steering wheels and a bell

But the best thing that we made
Were an old skate and a book
As we zoomed of down the Montrose Road
And all the parked cars were overtook

Now our John he were the fastest
Round the lamp post and the telegraph pole
Till we heard his cries of anguish
The gasmen had dug a hole

John he laid there roaring
Cause the skate had hit the crack
But the gasmen came out all the worse
With wheel marks up his back.

Melvyn Mather

'GOD SAVE US ALL' SAID GREAT AUNT NELL

The aunts sat round the table, to glean what light they could,
Young Ida sat before the grate and watched the spitting wood,
Black Tom flexed out his killing claws and dreamed of golden cream,
And the paraffin lamp licked up its flame and shadows danced the beam.
The ageing eyes peered closely and the mending hooks stitched on,
The factory smell of oil and lint from the work skips lingered on,
The aunts sang loud their chapel hymns as all good ladies should,
And the lamp shone like a beacon on a sea of polished wood.
The pendulum of the kitchen clock pulsed from its clockwork heart,
The kettle on the blacklead hob keened its song in part,
Young Ida dreamed the burning caves and walked the paths of fire,
And the searching flame in the polished glass saw the menders work stack
                                                              higher.
The black tinned hands of the German clock pointed the hour of ten,
Young Ida hopes she'd been forgotten and would stay up late again
The chapel ladies hooks tacked on as they walked that 'Beautiful Shore',
But the evil thing from the black of night lifted the latch of the door.
The winter's cold came to their midst, their pious voices stilled,
Cold fingers touched young Ida's face, her very soul was chilled,
Black Toms fur stood end on end, the truth to God I'll tell.
The kitchen clock smashed to the floor, 'God save us' said Aunt Nell.
Black Tom was stretched as on a rack, then with a clap of thunder,
The oil lamp flame reached to the roof and the table split asunder.
The old oak slab divided, but how I'll never prove,
As the factory work fell to the floor, the oil lamp didn't move.
Half a century later, young Ida's tale I tell,
Just one tongue could find its speech, 'God save us' said Aunt Nell.
Their frozen fingers crossed their hearts, their throats were choked with
                                                              pain,
When without a sound or a splinter of wood, the oak was joined again.
The door latch clicked, the flame went down, the night 'Thing' took its
                                                              spell,
But the broken clock was on the ground, 'He's saved us' said Aunt Nell . . .

Brian Simpson

SUNDAY SCHOOL OUTING TO THE BLACK COUNTRY MUSEUM

Oh! What a day it was going to be as we all set off for the Black Country.
Our first treat in store was a ride in a tram, no traffic about to get stuck in a
                                                                                    jam.
The guide was dressed in olden clothes, bright neckerchief, waistcoat,
                                                                    boots and hose.
He showed us where limestone was mined, canals where the long boats
                                                                    bravely wind.
Where chains were made and rolling mills, the bakery where bread's made
                                                                    still!
Cottages just how they used to be, with black hearth and a copper, a sight
                                                                    to see.
The chemist shop where pills were made, rows of bottles in mysterious
                                                                    shades.
The grocer's full of wonderful things, rinso, liberty bodices, pins.
The chapel so warm and inviting to stay, to feel God's presence, to sit and
                                                                    pray.

We went on a boat ride through caves very dark, it was rather creepy but
                                                                    for some quite a lark.
A fabulous day we had all in all, and the Good Lord never let any rain fall.
For our safe journey home we gave thanks to the Lord, in that we were all
                                                                    in one accord.

Patricia Lamb

80

ALL IN THE MIND

A little girl saw fairies
Beside a hollow tree
With silver threads around it
My wonderful memory.
It was so very pretty
As far as I recall,
Unlike the things I see today,
Rude writings on the wall.
We sang the hymns together
While bathing by the fire,
Sundays now for shopping
Will hardly help inspire.
Some people think I'm silly
Perhaps they could be right
But I see the future
Not particularly bright.
What ever kind of values
Do people have today
Is it only money?
Difficult to say.
If love could only conquer
All disputes young and old,
There would be warmth around us
Instead of feeling cold.

Audrey Hoysted

THE OLD GRANDFATHERS CLOCK

The old grandfathers clock stands so lonely in the hall,
Where it chimes out the hours, every day
the maid dusts the fading wood, where
so many people have touched it, as they
stood waiting for their carriages.

Time has gone by quickly, and the days
have turned into years.
But still a maid dusts, the old grandfathers
clock that stands so lonely in the hall.

There's no more carriages waiting outside,
Just the modern motor cars,
No horses on old cobbled stones, as the
carriages used to do.
But still the old grandfathers clock, stands
so lonely in the hall, where the maid still
dusts the fading wood.

M Connolly

A CUP OF TEA

Funny, upon getting up, it seems for most of us, the day usually starts, with a steaming boiled kettle to infuse, the much sort after tea.

The clinking of the cups and saucers.

The longing for such a thirst quencher, all happens upon the first mouthful, and the downing of such.

With a usual 'Ah! I wanted that' such a small thing, but one that brings such pleasure.

Upon having visitors, one of the first questions asked is would they like a cup of tea or some other beverage.

Nine times out of ten, a cup of tea, is the first choice, such a handed down procedure, and I suppose it always will be,

In the future generations to come, as well.

Jean Dickens

THE LORD'S RAP

Our Father who art in heaven hallowed be Thy name
If I said 'Hey Dad, I love you loads,' do you think it'd be the
same?

Thy kingdom come - Thy will be done on earth as it is in
heaven
Well I'll do what you say and putting peace in my way I'll avoid
the Deadly Seven!

Give us this day our daily bread - so feed us like there's no
tomorrow.
And forgive us all our trespasses when we come to you in
sorrow.

But only forgive as we forgive those bums who shit upon us.
For giving gives freedom that we might live and love them
though they wrong us.

And lead us not into temptation but deliver us from sin
'cause we are easily led astray to the messes we get in.

For Thine is the kingdom, the power and the glory
for ever and ever, Amen.

And it's just as well - I don't want no Hell
so I'll pray this prayer again!

Sue Walker

WOMAN TO WOMAN

If the earth could talk what would she say?
'Did you know, I am like you in many a way.'
'But I have a child, you have none.'
'Oh no. I have many more than one,
all mine are planted in the ground,
while yours are free to run around.'
'But mine can think and understand
and yours is just a timberland.
No brain, no heart, they are just - wood.
I thought that this was understood.'
'So wrong, so wrong. They think of you,
leaves take your breath and make it new.
Their hearts are in the fruit they bear
and everything, with you they share,
warmth and shelter all this they bring
and so much beauty in the spring.
Their seeds they drop into my earth.
Then just like you I give birth.'

J R Williams

THE LONELY PEOPLE

She sits alone there every night,
Looking such an awful sight,
No make-up on and hair just lank,
Her mind is just an awful blank,
For all it seems is toil and worry,
And folk go by in such a hurry,
No time to stop and just be kind.
Surely they can't all be blind?
But they pass by without a care,
They never really see her there.

Tricia Watling

LOVE OF MY LIFE

Around six each morning,
I'm woken by their kisses,
To lie in till seven,
Is one of my greatest wishes.
But they want breakfast,
Every morning on the dot,
And before going walking,
Vitamins mustn't be forgot.
Then whilst their resting,
I do housework at fast pace,
For once those eyes open,
It'll be football or chase.
All too soon time for tea,
So store games in the shed,
Just time for a little TV
Before tucking them into bed.
Yes it's true they rule me,
Sometimes cause me strife,
But my American Cocker Spaniels,
Are the love of my life . . .

Sandra Austin

THOUGHTS

I am alone in my soul
No-one can see within
No-one knows the loneliness
No-one knows the sin
Of loving only one man
I wait forever for him.

Norma Allender

TO MY HUSBAND MIKE

I sit at night alone in bed,
I think about the things we said,
The happy times, and the sad,
Oh! how it makes me mad,
To think about things that we had done,
Please tell me where, I went wrong,
The good, the bad, the in-between,
Why is life so very mean?
But life goes on without a doubt,
But all I want is to scream and shout,
'Leave me alone, I've done no wrong',
Let life go on and keep me strong,
For the kids I ask and pray,
Life gets better everyday.

Heather Ball

A NEW TOMORROW

Don't look back look forward
Tomorrow's a brand new day
Don't be too downhearted
If things haven't gone your way

Everyone has ups and downs
Good times and the sorrow
So if your day has been dull and grey
The sun may shine tomorrow

They say tomorrow never comes
In fact we know that's right
We hope until the end of time
Day will follow night

Hilda Phillips

A QUESTION OF POETRY

What is poetry, an art, a science, a craft;
to write it do you need to be intelligent or does it help if you're a little daft?
Is poetry a profession or a hobby;
penned by qualified folk or jotted down by anybody?
Who is a poet, somebody who sits and contemplates for very long;
or a person who can quickly write the lyrics to a song?
Are poets privileged and gifted or ordinary people off the street;
writing of experiences including love, however sickly and sweet?
Is a poem something that has to be intellectual, profound and serious;
or can it be simple, uncomplicated and curious?
Does it need to rhyme, tell a story or just be a ditty;
make you laugh, cry or be happy and witty?
Should it be written in a library on expensive parchment with ink and quill;
or is it acceptable to write it on a bus on the back of an old shopping bill?
Are all of these things permissible and more;
something that excites and helps to open another door?
Should there be any rules or restrictions;
or can subjects be a matter of fact or fictitious predictions?
The answers to the questions, maybe there are none;
does it really matter as long as it's enjoyed by someone!

Charles Richard Gurden

EASTER

Easter is a joyous time - spring flowers and blossom fair,
Chocolate eggs and holidays and weddings everywhere.
God wants us to be happy and enjoy all He has made,
To trust His gracious promises and never be afraid.

So, what does Easter signify? So many do not know -
That lives can be transformed and love and joy can overflow.
So let us ponder for a moment, visualising what took place,
And thanking God for all His tender mercy and His grace.

Palm Sunday was the day when Jesus was acclaimed as King.
As He rode into Jerusalem the crowds began to sing -
'Blessed is the King that cometh, peace in Heaven, too,
And glory in the highest.' All they acclaimed was true.

His followers were praising God for all they'd seen Him do.
They spread palm branches on the ground and many garments too.
The Pharisees were angry as they heard the people shout,
But Jesus said that if they stopped, the stones would then cry out.

He cast men from the temple, who were there to buy and sell,
Then taught disciples daily and the people listened well.
The chief priests and the scribes were angry - they were fearful, too.
How could they destroy this man who knew them through and through?

Jesus taught in parables - His listeners were amazed
He told them what would happen on the earth in latter days.
He told them to be watching, ready at any hour
For when the Son of Man returns in glory and in power.

So, on Good Friday we remember Jesus, God's dear Son,
And how, through Him, eternal life and victory were won.
For He was led to Calvary, there to be crucified,
Bearing your sin and mine, He hung in anguish, bled and died.

Ivy Nurse

BOOTS

Cowboy boots in films pose
China boots with a rose
Stone boots full of flowers
Coloured wellie boots in showers

Knitted boots for a baby
Dainty ankle boots for a lady
Trainer boots expensive elite
To spur on the athlete

Pantomime boots up to the thigh
Sturdy walking boots up hills high
Dr Martin boots at school
Fur-lined boots in weather cool

Football boots muddy, torn
Work boots scruffy well worn
Steel toe cap gleaming
Polished boots soldiers marching

Ski boots gliding to cheers
Hob nail boots of past years
Now thick rubber sole to last
Roller boots whizzing past

Motor bike boots Hells Angels
Boots for Tug of War, not sandals
Jodhpur boots riding horses to win
Some useful boots to step out in.

Mary Mycock

MY FATHER

My father was a miner
Worked all his life in the pit,
He came from humble beginnings
And was not known for his wit.

But he did his bit in the army
And was the father of four,
Honest, kind and faithful
He never lusted for more.

Nothing was too much trouble
For he treated everyone the same,
But when my brothers were naughty
It was always me got the blame.

We all had chores to do at home
And did them at the double,
Heaven forbid if we forgot
Then we would be in trouble.

He took us to the seaside once
We played all day in the sea,
Then off back to a caravan
With bread and jam for tea.

And then he had an accident
It happened down the mine,
A fractured skull and blindness
But you never heard him whine.

They finished him at sixty
He was a smashing bloke,
He'd potter around his garden
And do jobs for other folk.

Dad never put his arms round us
Or kissed us when we cried,
But we knew that he loved us all
Until the day he died.

Christine Coulson

SANDY'S EDALE

We walked along a path
You and I,
With cobbled stones beneath
the sky,
The heather green and crisp
by cold,
The hills they stand there
strong and bold,
The stream which runs
like life itself
from hilltop to the soul
it delves,
This place untouched by
human hands
You have to stop and take
a stand,
And let your eyes intake
of this
A masterpiece of art and bliss,
So I will not forget my friend
this place of yours and your
content
Where you now walk your spirit
free.
Where you will always be for me!

Carol McGowan

NIGHT AND DAY

Crisp, still, icy nights,
With a clear, starlit sky,
The silence only broken,
By owls, as they fly.

Past yonder hill far away,
Morning makes its mark,
Gently gives a warming glow,
Giving lightness to the dark.

Within an hour, the sun is up,
And golden rays shine down.
It melts the frost that ol' Jack left,
From the roof tops of our town.

R P Williams

A LIGHT IN THE DARK

It's easy enough to keep smiling
When the road is happy and gay
When the view all around is lovely
And fortune lights our way

But the smile that's worth remembering
Is the one when things go wrong
So practice your smile in the sunshine
And meet the clouds with a song

Have a patient ear and kindly heart
Ready with a helping hand
A gentle voice and kindly eye
That's quick to understand

What joy you will spread to others
From darkness into light
So take a friendly candle
Into someone's lonely night.

Maud

A BAD RIDE HAME

I was on a plane,
going back hame.
When I noticed my ma wasny there.
I was scared,
I was frightened.
But I did nae cry 'cause I'm big noo
and that's nae lie.

I waited for aboot ten minute.
Then I went up tae the man whi
the roond bonnet,
I said tae him very politely,
excuse me sir when will I be hame.
He said something but I did nae understan it.

I had nae money, nae claes,
but the worst thing was nae ma.
I did nae ken where I was or where I was gaine.
So when we landed I was stranded,
and I did nae ken whit tae dae.

I thought I was in Edinburgh,
so I went tae see if there were any coppers.
I saw a copper whi a hat on,
so I went up tae him
my ma whis in front ae him.

I was sae happi and meh hoose
whis just doon the road.
Mi ma never did tell me
whit plane whe was on.

Rachel Milne

THE LOVERS

Be - still - our hearts,
As - now - we - part,
Two - lovers - clinging,
In - sweet - embrace,
Dreaming - of - the - new - tomorrow,
When two - hearts - joined - together,
Will - sing - love's - sweet - song,
Through - any - weather.

Thus - dawn's - the - day,
And - now - she - may,
Put - on - the - lovely - bridal array,
To - meet - her - dear - lover,
And - truly - say, - beloved - mine,
This - is - our - lovely - day,
Our - wonderful - wonderful,
Eagerly - waited - for - wedding day

The - organist - plays,
Hear - Comes - The Bride,
Sweet - bells - chime,
As - she - steps - to - his - side,
Vows - truly - spoken,
Our - Father - above,
Addeth - His - blessing,
On - their - mutual - love.

Kathleen Willis

MY INSPIRATION
(Dedicated to Rabbie Burns)

When I was small I read a poem
That fascinated me.
Who was this man who wrote these words
Who could this person be?

So full of thought and such emotion
His soul he had laid bare.
Now here I was inside his heart
Through words he's written there.

I asked my teacher who he was
And where he lived these days
She said his day was years ago
And he'd long since passed away.

I felt quite sad and yet was honoured.
His tender words to read
And this man of thoughts from long ago
Left in my mind a seed.

Now when I write of many things
Of life and love's sensations
I know that he will always be
My source of inspiration.

Maranna Hutton

TELL ME FATHER IN HEAVEN

Tell me Father why do we cry?
All the pain drains us dry
We pray and pray for you to hear,
Is there a heaven?
Yes plain and clear,
We all are your children you love us dear,
You have given us angels dear,
To pass the prayer loud and clear.
You heal if you can,
If not we come home to you,
We give thanks to you, to hear you say
I walk with you.
No more pain and fear
We've seen the light
Heaven shining bright.
No more tears you wipe them away.
Then we know you've heard our prayers.

Maria

A MOMENT OF LAUGHTER

I pushed and pulled but the shoe wouldn't fit,
Mum creased up laughing, unable to sit.
The shoe went flying up into the air,
Landing in the corner by the old chair.
One shoe fitted, but the other did not
I was getting so angry, flushed and hot.
I seethed! What's wrong with that stupid old shoe,
My mind boggled, I hadn't got a clue.
I picked up that old shoe and I shook it
Then I saw with my eyes why it wouldn't fit,
For there at the tip where the big toe dwells,
Was an old sock full of yesterday's smells!

Mary McSweeney

I DREAMT OF DADDY LAST NIGHT

I dreamt of daddy last night,
I dreamt of fun and games.
There were lots of people everywhere,
but I did not know their names.

I dreamt of daddy last night,
we were playing in the sand.
Then mummy came to take us home,
and we walked off hand in hand.

I dreamt of daddy last night,
he was there to end my fears.
But when I woke this morning,
my pillow was full of tears.

J E Quigley

MARTIN

We have a wee grandson
A great wee guy
He's cute and he's handsome
And he kids on he's shy
If your feeling fed up
Or just feeling down
He will give you a smile
Never a frown
He is very special
Well we think he is
He looks so cute
I must give him a kiss
I'm sure he'll be saying
Well! I almost would bet
Oh no! Here comes my nanny
To make my face wet.

Margaret Curran

UNTITLED

Birdies, pars, holes in one.
The weekend's here and off he's gone.
Up at dawn without a sound,
Creeping out for another round.
Cleaning his clubs with great precision,
Selecting a ball's a major decision.
Clubs in hand, he's out of the door,
Hoping to beat, last week's score.
Playing at courses near and far,
I'm stuck at home, without the car.
Hitting his drive off the 1st tee,
Chatting to pals, never thinking of me.
Shots going wide and missing the flag,
Throwing the clubs into the bag.
The 19th hole, they all have a drink,
Discussing the putts that they tried to sink.
Waiting at home, I hope he played well,
Is it going to be peace or going to be hell?
Coming up the path, at the window I stare
Has he a smile or a terrible glare?
During the week at the driving range,
Trying new things, he's going to change.
Reading golf books to get some new tips,
Learning to putt and practising chip.
Talking of shots that cost so dearly,
The ones he played, that were oh so nearly.
Woods, irons, Faldo, fore and ping,
I just wish he'd stop, the whole bloody thing.

Stephanie Parkin

SECOND BEST

Ah! Dreams, dreams,
Where would I be
Without dreams?
What would I be?
I would be ageing,
Not forever young.

Looking through these eyes,
In my dreams, whilst
All around is changing
I remain the same.

Secret loves flit and fly
Through my world.
Adventures come and go.
I never know when
I will be put to the test.

I slip into my bed.
Slip into my dreams
And settle for second best!

Peter Oates

GOOGLE TEX

Google Tex is my dragon beast,
He loves to eat a good old feast,
He went off to town one day,
These people came and took him away,
I searched for him till I was blue in the face,
My dragon used to be an ace.

Manjinder Dhillon

MAIG

There's a special kind of feeling
That's really hard to say
But in my heart are the memories
That's loved and cherished, every single day

To me you were something special
You gave me all you had to give
Of a life and times remembered
For as long as I have to live

I treasure all the memories
Of some days that used to be
the happy songs, that you would sing
And of the gladness, they gave to me

Life for you was painful
my love for you was there
No one ever knows the sadness
When I speak to you in prayer

Our special years cannot return
Those days are in the past
They hold a million memories
Of the times, that will always last

My heart still aches with sadness
Where silent tears still flow
But in my heart, you're always there
Where no one else can go

Lewis Morrison Gray

GREEN WATERS

Come into the water where it's cool and deep,
so placid and tranquil it makes you weep
as you float on the surface away from the shore,
while inside emotions are fighting a war.
Half wants to dive down, be engulfed by the swell
while the other is cautious and constantly tells
you to turn around now while no harm has been done
despite that you think you would maybe have fun.
So you drift for a while and consider these thoughts
but without really knowing that you've actually been caught
as the current is pulling you deep down inside
you know that the waters have blatantly lied.
They're not as you thought, so peaceful and mild
but constantly churning, emotions so wild
that you can't understand how you just didn't know
of the passion calm waters have hidden below.
So next time you see that the green waters rise
and find that you're looking deep into my eyes,
swim into the depths and I'm sure you will find
you won't want to leave the cool waters behind.

Marianne Joslin

HELL

I'm sorry daddy, mummy dear
I have to get away from here
I don't know any other way
I can't go back there one more day
They hurt me every single week
I dream of them while I'm asleep
They pull my hair, spit in my face
and hurt me in a private place
They do this to me every day
My friends can only look away
Why always me I want to know
What have I done to be hurt so?
My pocket money they take away
'Bring in some more', they always say
I'm sorry dad for what I've done
I had to steal it from you mum
They said they'd kill me if I tell
those school gates are the gates of hell
It's not your fault it's them to blame
Inside my bag are all their names
I was afraid to say before
but they can't hurt me anymore
Don't cry for me don't cry for me
I'm happy now at last I'm free
I had to get away from here
I'm sorry daddy, mummy dear

Dominic McCallion

TO LIZZIE

We've been friends for many years
Through times of happiness
And times of tears
Friends through and through
I think that describes
Me and you

Cheering me up you did so well
If I was unhappy you could tell
Through trouble and strife
Your a friend for always
A friend for life

And now you walk on new ground
Because the love you seek
You have now found
You deserve the very best
Love, happiness and all the rest

So, take care from me to you
A friend always, through and through.

Janice McGilvray

THE MESSAGE OF EASTER

I left the church on Easter Day.
The service had been grand.
I met a friend who said to me
'I cannot understand,
This talk of Jesus dying, then rising from the tomb,
What proof is there this came about?
You've got an answer I assume
Or do you sometimes doubt?'
'Have you heard that saying', I replied
'About being too blind to see?
The answer comes to us each spring
With every flower and leaf and tree.
Each plant is dead all winter through,
There's stillness in the land,
But then one day they bloom again
At some unseen command.
We humans plant the greenery
But only *He* can make them grow
And if *He* wished it otherwise
They wouldn't even show.
And this is proof as each spring comes
That death is not the end.
So look around you every spring,
The answer's there my friend.'

Jean Donaghue

CANTERBURY

Canterbury, ancient city
Cathedral soaring high
Towers filled with faded standards
Reminding us of days gone by.

When royal kings would lead their armies
Into battle 'gainst the foe
Pennons waving in the breeze
As standards make so brave a show.

Relics of those bygone days
There for all of us to see
Reminders of the brave and glorious
Ages in our history.

Within your walls will there be whispers
From valiant heroes old and new?
Calling from our glorious past
To keep the memories ever new.

Canterbury, ancient city
In the years to come
Will future generations see
More recent deeds by England's sons.

Edna Cosby

IN THE COUNTRYSIDE

The walker on the muddied track
Sees life with every measured tread.
He breathes sweet air, the scent of hay,
Or the rank sharpness of the milking shed.
His face is washed with rain and feels
The sun and wind upon his cheek.

His friends are the frisky lambs in spring,
Bearded goats, bad-tempered geese,
And the ass behind the orchard hedge.
His heart is gladdened by wood violets,
Primroses in clumps, anemones and celandines.
He shuffles through drifts of autumn leaves
Where mushrooms, beechnuts and acorns hide.

Smooth green downs entice him to climb
Rough, springy turf; 'til at the crest
He sees another hill, another beechen copse.
Midday will find him, slouching wearily
Across the car park to the public bar
And the chilled amber pint that's his reward.

Drivers inside their metal coffins
Peer through windscreens and see
Only a hundred yards of carriageway.

Tom Wilson

WAITING FOR SPRING

I'm waiting for the cuckoo to call in the woods,
I'm waiting for the flowers to show their buds,
For the cold to vanish with its ugly face,
I'm waiting for spring to take its place,

For the sun to shine and warm the ground,
To caress each single hill and mound,
For the birds to start to build their nest,
For new life to begin, and be our guest,

Each day grows lighter and longer in spring,
Those sweet little songs that all the birds sing,
The first bees and butterflies, fresh on the wing,
I'm waiting, I'm waiting, for spring.

Sandra Hemingway

FAST PACE

Rising early in the morning
I am late no time to talk
Hurry to the car, wheels turning
Traffic jams no space to sport.
Phone call can you go to Oxford
Opposite way to which I sought
Hundred miles of black track sleeking
Meeting cancelled stress a creeping.
Go to Bournemouth, other places
Wheels a turning seeking spaces
2pm no time to eat
Further meeting time to keep
Listen to broadcast what's that they say
Travel by bus it's the easier way
No life style considered or how business is run
Do committees think that our life is just fun?

Jane Darnell

A SINGLE ROSE

A single rose, oh yes, thee outstanding one.
My rose, my rose, I love your sweet pose,
The sweetest flower that ever grows,
You need, no care, just lovely fresh air,
And I love you, my rose, my rose,
Like a single rose in the garden,
More lovely than the rest,
It has a special beauty,
Found only in the best,
Such roses are always kept
As they are very few,
You bloom all alone,
And stand out on your own so true,
When other flowers die they leave you still there,
Shining bright, till dawn and midnight,
My rose, my rose, what a wonderful sight,
As a single rose in the garden,
That's how I think of you.

William Robert Deaves

SMALL TALK

No-one to talk to, live on my own.
Natter to radio, reach for the 'phone.
Ladies in library, have a brief chat.
The bus driver sings to us - how about that?
People on trains do not often talk
But if you've a dog, folks will chat when you walk.
I may get a budgie and teach him to speak.
The heart is quite willing but the flesh is so weak!
Yet - I can still hear, with specs I can see,
Sure there are some folks worse off than me,
So gab on old girl, and never give up.
There's no one to say 'Please, will you shut up?'

Betty Dwyer

DEPRESSED AND ALL ALONE

I feel different
Alone in an empty room
No one to talk to
Just me and dusty broom
I want to be ordinary
But that can not be
I feel different
Oh why oh why me?

I feel like a tree
On a lonely hillside
With no birds in my branches
To play and hide
I want to be ordinary
But that cannot be
I feel different
Oh why oh why me?

Trapped in a universe
All alone
What can I do to get back home?
I want to be ordinary
But that can not be
I feel different
Oh why oh why me?

I've found a friend
Who understands
We play together in the sands
Now I am ordinary
As you can see
We are one of a kind
Me and thee.

Helena Sillitoe

WHITE MAGIC

I have wakened in a different world
Halted calmed and still
Motionless and chilling
Is there a town over the hill
Transport has been muffled
Not a car in sight
Where have all the people gone?
Wasn't like this last night
Scenes no longer recognisable
Familiar shapes look strange
Akin to an alien planet
All scenario re-arranged
Everything lies sleeping
A hush hangs o'er the land
Nature having gone to rest
And beauty in command
What's caused this transformation?
As if you didn't know
The land is nestling 'neath a shawl
A pure blanket made of snow

Winifred Smith

THIRD WORLD BOY

A lonely boy,
A lonely city,
Lonely road, always gritty,
Soles of his shoes are worn right through,
Outstretched arms calling to you,
All he needs is someone to care,
All he needs is someone to share,

Lonely boy,
Lonely city,
Lonely road, always gritty,
Soles of his shoes are brand new,
In his prayers he's thanking you,
All he needed was someone to care,
All he needed was someone to share,
You gave him hope, to go on in his world,
A far cry from your home sweet home,

He may be, frail and dying,
In his heart, he may be crying,
But knowing that somebody cares enough,
To share their love and take their time,
To give him something new,   .
He will always be thanking you.

Shelley Corbett

RENA'S PARTY

In a place called Lochore, at the foot of Benarty.
Rena came from America, for her 70th party.
We arrived there at six, at the institute hall.
The balloons and the banners were up on the wall.

The meal was delicious, the service was good.
Soon all the guests were enjoying the food.
The tables were cleared, the food was all done.
We moved to the side all prepared for the fun.

The band got set up, they started to play.
By now Rena's party was well on the way.
We got out the camera. But what will we take.
Some photos of Rena cutting her cake.

They brought out a buffet, it all looked so good.
The band had a break, while we ate the food.
We had a few singers, and some dancing too.
Soon the party was over, we felt quite blue.

Thanks to Jean and to Rena, the night had gone fine.
To soon we were singing for Auld Lang Syne.
The whole night was good, the food, music and beer.
Special thank you to Jeannie, so give her a cheer.

A Murray

WILD GEESE

The skeins of geese, like streamers,
      fly past, in the sky
And when the gaggling birds pass,
      another skein comes by.
To fill the evening sky with magic
      for the eye
Holding us in wonder, and joy
      for you and I.

We here, in Norfolk, are truly blessed,
      that we know.
To look up at the setting sun
      sinks low, and so -
Find a quiet spot and wait till
      the time that we know
When the geese will come in arrows,
      and untidy row.

Our eyes set on high, and with
      aching necks, indeed,
As countless numbers fly past us
      in urgent need.
To search, and find the muddy flats
      and wind-lashed reed,
A place to rest their weary wings,
      and then, to feed.

Joan Adams

MOTHER EARTH

The Earth is tired
She's had enough
of man's abuse
it's so injust.

She gave her all
There was enough
But greed and need
got all mixed up.

We haven't learned
to give and take
Man likes to
Have it all one way.

One day the earth
Will sadly die
With no-one left
To wonder why.

Shirley Leonard

THE WORLD

There is pain all over the world.
Some people are crying
While others are dying.
There are people selling drugs on the streets
Which any kid could meet.
There are children smoking in the schools
Because they think it looks rather cool.
Or they get them self drunk in the night
And sometimes end up in a fight.
I think the world is so bad
And it makes me feel so sad.
If only they all could know
That there is someone there.
Someone who really does care.
Someone who wants to help you and me
And help us all to see
His name is Jesus Christ
he can brighten up our lives
So give him a go.
And you will soon know
That he is the best
Better than anything else.

Rebecca Dey (16)

SNAKES ALIVE!

We were all aht walkin' rahnd Bilsdale Way.
It were nice an' sunny - a lovely day,
When all on a sudden a snake wi spied.
Wi were rooited ter t'spot, wi nearly died.
It were just laid theer on some grass.
Wi stood an' wi gawped, ter freetened ter pass.

Then ar little Emma in tremblin' voice
Sez 'Ah think it's a cobra, wid best not get cloise'.
'It i'n't, yer daft thing', whispered ar Nellie,
'It's one o' them vipers, ah've seen 'em on't telly.'
'Ooh lawks! it's a python', screeamed Janette
In a blood-curdlin' voice ah'll nivver forget.

Then Jim from next door, ter keeap us all calm,
Sez 'It's only a grass snake, it'll do us no 'arm'.
Befoor any o't others cud 'ev their say
T'snake just ups an' slithers away.
So when wi gor 'ooam wi asked Steve's fadder
An' ee sez 'Well, yer all wrong, yon were an adder!'

Ellen Barber

THE CASTLE ON TOP OF THE HILL

There is an ancient castle on tope of the hill,
Where the wind whistles through with an eerie chill.
And there lives an old lady all on her own,
They say at her local that she likes to have a moan,
About bats in the belfry and spiders in the hall,
And a skeleton or two behind a secret wall.
When the full moons-a-glowing casting its gentle light,
Shadows start to move in the dead of night.
Noises do abound and footsteps come and go,
'Orrible groans are heard that sound so full of woe,
Chains start a rattling along the corridors,
Then ghostly apparitions float across the floors.
No one ventures to the castle on top of the hill,
No letter from the waterboard or electricity bill.
No final demands sent to give a scare,
Just the odd invitation to some charity affair.
I often wonder about that sly old girl,
If she's sitting there laughing giving is all a whirl.
Or if ghosts and ghoulies really do run amuck,
I'll just have to wonder rather than test out my luck.
With twinkling eyes she gives is such a thrill,
Telling tales of her ancient castle on top of the hill.

Alex I Askaroff

UNKNOWN

My frame is small, my hair is grey,
But you can't judge a book, by the cover they say.
My outside appearance, may deceive you at first;
But inside my brain had a terrible thirst.
It's not for liquids that I desire,
But for much greater things that I aspire.
       This feeling inside me, has taken a hold;
I'm going to write poems and be very bold.
This urge I have, won't go away;
Tucked in my brain, I have so much to say.
       The words have laid dormant, for such a long time;
Now all of my quotes are turning to rhyme.
       So when I am working, and feeling depressed;
I write down my feelings, that have been so suppressed:
       I am filled with excitement, turmoil, and fear;
If I write what I am thinking, will you want to hear?

Joan Harding

BREATH OF SPRING

Daffodils nodding their heads,
knowing everything that's being said,
about the weather;
and lengthening days.
The gentle wind with its blustery way.
swaying everything to and fro,
hoping there will be no more snow
to bend their heads to the ground.
So they hear no more sound.
And as the sun warms the wind
and the birds start to sing
What a joy for each living things
to feel the warm breath of spring.

Molly Barsby

BLOSSOMS OF BOSNIA

Evil shadows passing through town and village.
Stopping to murder women, children rape and pillage.
Gaunt faces go by, no noise, there's just a leer.
They're not wanted amidst Blossoms of Bosnia.

Women and children buried on the hill.
In neat rows, no birds sing, all is still.
During dark hours, on each grave will appear.
Sprigs of flowers, the Blossoms of Bosnia.

Who is doing these deeds? I stand and shout.
No answer is heard, what's it all about?
Disgruntled I walk away, in my eyes a tear.
At least I see the Blossoms of Bosnia.

Can some good people set all of us free?
Though that seems far away from our reality.
A miracle would be too late for most I fear.
So make the most of the Blossoms of Bosnia.

Then comes the wicked chatter of some ones gun.
I fall face down in the morning sun.
My spirit rises to the atmosphere.
Now even I cannot see the Blossoms of Bosnia.

C F Armstrong

ESTA NOOATICED

Esta nooaticed ar things ev changed sich a lot
Ovvert years sin wi wor much younger an strong
Not awny things but fooak an all
Even them wi move abart daily among

Ivvry things farther away than afore
It's twice as far nar darn tat shops
Ar find it's steeaper nar back up that hill
An am fooarced ter mak wun a two stops

Ev yer nooaticed at tellys quieter nar
An mooast fooak seem ter talk low
Yer find if yer dooant ask em ta spaik up
Wot they said yer'll nivver just know

Print in paper is gerrin sooa small
Yer can hardly read wots written neat
An ar find winter neets much coder nar
It's wool socks in bed for mi feet

Last week ar met Billy art a my class at schooil
An he'd aged a gret lot ar cud see
A lot moor na me as ar peeped ovver mi specs
An it wor plain he couldn't place me.

As ar commed wot wor left of mi hair this morn
Ar wundered wal stannin theer sa brave
Why mi parting an waves wor nar just 'slippy top'
Ar wor it ar wor still fooarced ter shave.

T Shaw

BROTHER TO BROTHER AGED 70

At the sign of the swinging crutches
By the sound of the hearing aid
Let's worship medical science
Gigantic strides they've made

With heart restarts and transplants
Replacement knees and hips
Blood replacement and of course
The swinging saline drips

Keyhole ops and laser beams
Complete change - forsooth
Not geriatrics any more
But full recycled youth

No slings or rampant zimmer frames
Can stop us getting through
And so, weather permitting
We're coming to your do.

B Drury

BLYTHBURGH CHURCH

When my steps falter
In life's relentless run,
I think of Blythburgh,
Where the angels dwell
And spread their wings of peace.
Where faithful Jack
Rings out his bell
To guide the weary home.
Where tired eyes
Chasing shadows through the night
Find joy,
to see your bright, enduring light.

Ron Ellis

AFTER THE STORM

The night was all noise with thunder and rain.
Now all is calm with snow in the lane
Piled high up the sides, on top of the hedges
And children rising down slopes on their sledges.
For now is the lull after the storm.
O what a contrast this beautiful morn.

Crystals shine in the crusted snow
Hurting the eyes with a dazzling glow.
And seagulls wings a brilliant white
As they dip and soar in lazy flight.
Diamonds of dew in the glittering hedge.
And snowdrops peep out from a mossy ledge.

Flooded fields mirror the sky's azure tone
A single sheep stands serene and alone
Away from the flock upon the hill,
Scenting the air, peaceful and still.
Silence except for the cawing of rooks
And the crack of the ice beneath my boots.

A robin sits on a broken wall
Warming his feathers while snowflakes fall
Floating down in the gentle breeze,
Dislodging the snow from overhead trees.
And in the meadow, wild and free
A mad March hare leaps in glee.

Dorothy Steele

HOBBIES

I thought I'd have a hobby to while away the hours.
I wanted to try gardening but was allergic to the flowers.
So then I took up jogging but my trainers hurt my feet.
And when I tried to ride a horse, I couldn't keep my seat.
I thought that I'd try swimming but I sank just like a stone,
And when I tried hang gliding I felt lonely on my own.
I went to do aerobics but my body wouldn't bend.
I wanted to play tennis but I didn't have a friend.
I took up stamp collecting but my stamps just wouldn't stick.
I took a course on photography but my camera wouldn't click.
I was keen to go sailing but I felt all cold and wet,
And when I took up cooking my jellies wouldn't set.
So now when I have some spare time, I think I'll stay in bed.
Or maybe, yes, just maybe, I'll write poetry instead.

Valerie Brown

THE WEDDING

Her flowing dress and summer flowers,
Confetti falling down in showers.
Her father's arm she held so proud,
To love and honour is what she vowed.
She slowly turns to see his smile,
A private moment for a while.
The preacher then did join their hands,
And light fell on their wedding bands.
We all do stand and sing our praise,
Sentimental tears, fall on a haze.
My daughter, my friend is now a wife,
About to start her own new life.
Now joined together in wedded bliss
They seal their bond with a loving kiss.

Karen-Anne Williams

MY WINDY

My name is Mr Windy
I blow from place to place,
Although you can feel me,
You can never see my face.
I blow the flowers gently,
They sway to and fro.
I can blow much harder,
And make a sail boat go.
I make the trees rustle
And the leaves fall to the ground,
I rush around the corner,
Making a whistling sound.
Sometimes I'm very naughty,
I blow your brolly inside out,
I try to blow your feet off,
And blow your hair about.
And when I'm in an angry mood,
I blow fierce and strong,
But, then I get tired out,
And I can't keep blowing long.

Ruth Davies

A RAMBLERS TALE

To see the sun in a baby blue sky
And watch the fluffy clouds roll by
Feeling the warmth of the summer's heat
Makes my heart thump and miss a beat
To hear the bird's full throated song
To see them soar and watch them throng
To feel the wind rush upon my face
Makes me feel glad to be in this place
Watch the tall trees as they rustle and sway
See the leaves fall and be blown away
Smell the moist air and the grass full of dew
So glad I'm here walking with you
See the grey heavy clouds all around
So full of rain to feed the ground
Taste the drops so warm and sweet
What a magical time for us to meet
See the sky clear now there's some blue
A rainbow of love for me and you
Red, blue and yellow what a glorious sight
To end the day and start the night
But a crack of thunder says beware
And lightning strikes above in mid air
All is not well and all is not safe
Better make haste and be gone from this place
Alone I watch the sky turn blue
You have long since gone to someone new
But still I see wonder all around
And hope is there for all to be found

Susan Lee

TO WATCH TELLY OR NOT (THIS IS THE QUESTION)

I'm sure I'm one of the million,
Who shares this affliction,
But I'm sure if I try hard I'll have this problem beat,
And wean myself off gradually, watching Brookside and Coronation Street
Just think of all those hidden talents I might have
I could take up with all that spare time
Maybe writing poetry and some may even rhyme
Or how about knitting a trendy jumper
Not resembling any other but totally unique.

But hold on a minute - Who do I think I'm kidding?
I'd miss all the characters who have become an extended family
There's nothing quite like a soap opera
While enjoying the afternoon cup of tea.

So long live my hero Racquel from Coronation Street
As she always makes me feel clever
As she seems to have only one braincell.

R Hodgkinson

SCHOOL DAY

It's Friday at Henbury Court School
We are all doing *Maths*
Maths is easy and boring
Playtime was cold and miserable
Then it's *English*
English is fine if you have time
Coping with work and all that
Then learning spellings just like that
Dinner time, walking around with nothing to do
We eat our dinner
munch munch munch
chew chew chew

Ralph Kirk (11)

THE ODDITIES OF SPACE

My mind is blank like the oddities in space,
Like the moon and sun and all the human-race,
Like the rings which surround Saturn and all the milky-way,
Has Jupiter got an atmosphere is it night or is it day,
These questions that I think about and ask myself?
Would I like to go to Pluto would you dare even try?
Like the nebula and the stars and the rush of Haley's comet,
Like Venus, mars, Uranus has mercury got a summit?
Like the constellation of the stars which form Orion's name,
Is there people up on Neptune are they really just the same?
On earth there is a realm which forms a mighty kingdom,
I wonder if there's life elsewhere
Do they form their own domminium?

Glen Frost

OUT IN SPACE

It is funny here
and when you jump you go far
because you go into space
It is more slow
it is clear because you can't
see dark planets
you can go to the moon
but you can't go to Mars
because you will get burnt as toast
you will be alien toast
you might want to go to Mercury
But be careful
because it is dangerous
will it be alright?
I bet a tenner
you will not come back.

Jonathan Price (9)

MY HOMELAND

I see my homeland from across the sea
 longing in my heart the place I want to be
For islands life, a sense of being free
Oh! Take me back home to Orkney

Where there's no hustle or bustle plenty of time
To sit by the fire recite an old rhyme
No smog, no trees lots of green pastureland
Wanting for nothing everything at hand.

Where there's prehistoric ventures to find
Hidden caves made by mankind
Wrecks in the sea from the war I'm told
Lots of stories to wear from the old

I see my homeland a far reach from me
Across the Pentland's rough stormy sea
The magestic isles are a sight to see
That's why Orkney is the place for me.

Helen A Bain

HORROR

Horror is a frightful sight,
Things which come out in the night.
Bats which bug when flapping their wing,
Or ghosts which howl, growl and sing.
Creaking floor-boards in the hall,
Or Frankinstein who stands so tall.
Peoples' heads which spin around,
Or rotting bodies coming up from the ground.
Cobwebs hanging down from ceilings,
Or strange and very icy feelings.
Doors and windows which lock themselves,
Or being chased by goblins and elves.

Donna Glover

128

THAT'S LIFE (AFTER DEATH)
(HYPOCRISY)

'Such a nice bloke', was what they said,
When they were told that he was dead
'He loved a laugh, a pint, a joke,
A really inoffensive bloke'.

Why didn't they tell him that last week
And bring a blush into his cheek.
It really would have made his day
To hear them speak of him this way.

Perhaps next week, if he comes back,
They'll say, 'It's good to see you, Jack
We missed your laugh, and missed your jokes
You really were one of the blokes.

But it's too late, he can't be here,
So have your fags, and drink your beer.
Then look around, and drown your sorrow,
Could be your turn to go to-morrow.

So just sit down, and have a think
When someone comes in for a drink
Greet him with 'Good morning then'
Not that old moaner's here again.

D C Morris

HAVE YOU GOT A MUM LIKE MY MUM?

Have you got a mum like my mum
Who makes you eat your greens,
them horrible peas and cabbage
and the dreadful runner beans.

Have you got a mum like my mum
who claims *Cliff Richard's* great
I think she needs her head read
He's past his sell by date.

Have you got a mum like my mum
who sings when having a bath,
You all gather round the keyhole
and have a jolly good laugh.

Have you got a mum like my mum
who watches you when you sleep.
She thinks I cannot see her
she thinks I'm counting sheep.

Have you got a mum like my mum
She's definitely one of the best
If entering a competition
I know she'd beat the rest.

Have you got a mum like my mum
who loves me more each day,
I love you mum I really do
that's all I'm trying to say.

S Grant

BEAT THE BURGLAR

I'd love to open a window, to let in some fresh air,
I'd love to leave it open but I'd better be aware
that while I've gone out shopping burglar Bill may call
So I'll not leave that window open to assist him with his haul.

I'll put my post code on my goods, so Bill cannot hide them in the woods
but if he makes off to sell his swag,
the police will catch him it's in the bag,
no newspapers left hanging out
a tell tale sign no-one's about.

The very best way to beat crimes that rock the nation
always insist on identification,
Make a phone call before you let strangers in
To find out if your caller is genuine.

I'm quite scared he'll choose to call, when I am home alone,
will I yell or shout or make it to the phone,
dial 999 to say that he's about
but what worries me even more, with all the locks and chains upon my
door

if he gets in can I get out.

Should Bill be tempted to try my door when I am not there
well I should warn him that he'd better be aware
I have friends in the neighbourhood keeping a watchful eye
and whoever enters when not invited
can expect a four legged reply *woof.*

Patricia Steers

THE MEADOW

On the lea, meadow ladies gently graze
The calves close to their side
Sheep too, with their lambs
Yonder, the horses snort and sniff the breeze.

High in the air
The sky lark soars
Heavenward
Its song pouring out.

Rabbits scurry here
and there
A soaring kestrel seeks its prey
A vole hurries in the grass.

In the breeze,
The scent of
New mown hay
As the harvest is gathered.

Cattle gently low,
As they wind their way o'er the lea.
The summer sun
beats down.

M Elsworthy

TO BE A MINER

To be a miner it's a must
Breathing foul air and coal dust
Strong men have gone to waste at the pit
Clogging their lungs with dust and grit

Each breath of life, their lungs do fight
Gone is their strength, gone is their might
Once fresh faces, now pale and drawn
Gone is their life, gone is their brawn

Tribunals give percent worth a few bob
Comes the bad news. Take a light job
Shadows of their former self
On the scrap heap, on the shelf

Came the day they closed my pit
No more foul air, dust or grit
As I left through yon gate
My remaining years in fresh air. It was great

A few sad words I must say
Some mates never lived to see this day
I think of them with great pride and deep sorrow
For these gallant men there's no tomorrow

David Johnston

MY DRIVING TEST

I passed my driving test today,
I thought you'd like to know.
The weather wasn't very good,
I hoped it wouldn't snow.
I wasn't very nervous,
(Just shaking in my shoes)
Then I thought 'Well this is it
I either win or lose'

Off I went for a pre-test,
An hour isn't so long,
Except when you're dreading the next one
And are doing everything wrong.
We finally came to the test centre,
Out my examiner came,
He called me over, gave me a form
And said 'Please sign your name.'

Off we went along the road
I thought 'Well this is it.'
By this time I'd stopped shaking
And settled down a bit.
I did all that he asked me to
The best way I knew how
I glanced at the clock on the dash
And thought 'It's all over now'.

We stopped just where we started
He looked ready for a rest.
Before he went he turned to say
'My dear you've passed your test.'

K S Hackleton

IMAGINATION

At the bottom of the garden, where the grass grows long
There's a beautiful bird, with a beautiful song
His feathers are jewelled, they glow like a fire
And his voice is a wondrous heavenly choir.

At the bottom of the garden, where the grass grows long
Is a huge fiercesome tiger, so savage and strong
He's sleek and he's tawny, his teeth gleaming white
And his eyes like twin diamonds, they shine through the night.

At the bottom of the garden, where the grass grows long
Is an impudent monkey - his tail is so long
He swings through the bushes and chatters away
He teases the tiger - invites him to play

At the bottom of the garden, where the grass grows tall
An elephant lurks by the garden wall
A long swinging trunk and an ivory tusk
Can be seen through the gloom in the gathering dusk

At the bottom of the garden, where the pond lies asleep
A pirate ship sails through the dark murky deep
And the captain is waiting for you and for me
To kidnap and take us away out to sea

At the bottom of the garden, where the bushes are thick
There's a witch lies in wait, with a magic broomstick
A black cat with whiskers and long furry tail
A two headed toad and a big slimy snail

All these things in the garden are waiting for us
Till the end of the day, in the gathering dusk
When mummy comes calling us - 'Playtime is done'
And they all disappear with the red setting sun.

S Ralph

OUR DOONIE

The dine or doonie or duvet us the continental quilt.
The trade name indicated the place in which it is built.
'Cause I love the border country, and I wed a dashing Scot,
We bought the awick made doonie, and sing its praises quite a lot.
The doonie is a muckle poke of cambric closely woven,
And in the channels of the poke are feathers carefully chosen.
Our doonie has two covers, her needs are very few,
'Holmes-made' ones are exclusive, I can recommend my work to you!
Doonie sits upon the bed and overhangs each side,
Which is very very handy, when one has a scrow to hide.
Doonie is a loner and can stand up to any test,
With a mattress, sheet and pillow one snuggles down to rest.
The comfort is ethereal, the weight is always right,
No cold spots in the winter, no swelter on a summer's night.
So, 'Farewell to fluffy blankets',
They are a menace in disguise,
Fluff causes nasty nasal dripping and bulbous watery eyes.

Peggy Power-Holmes

REMEMBER

The blood red poppy worn with pride
Remembering young men and women who died.
Serving their country in far off land
They never hear the marching band.
Silence reigns as the bugles sound
And the fall of leaves upon the ground,
Grimfaced people watch and wait
The call to prayer by church and state.
Medals glint and arms swing out,
the white cenotaph as sergeants shout,
'Eyes left' they turn as one man
To honour the dead in a foreign land
Men in wheelchairs pass on by
Each stern-faced but bright of eye,
Wishing they could march along
As the band strikes up another song.
Holding on to another's hand
Sightless eyes at the command
Pay their tribute when 'Eyes left' is said
To 'see' the poppies oh so red
In history books this date will stay
As nations join as one to pray
Reminding each one of the terrible cost
To mothers, of the sons they lost.

M Russell

A MAYS DAY

Beneath the tree with cheese and wine
Two people sat in this dream of mine,
They each had a story to relate
They each had a need of an understanding mate.
As they spoke of the months gone past
Since they had been together last.
The cherished love of a sweet 'Mays Day'
Came flooding back and I heard her/him say -
You've been so good, so brave, so very good
You've been all that I hoped you would.
I've loved you long, I've loved you true,
'I've often wondered, if you loved me too.'
She sighed and lifted her eyes to his
She placed on his lips a lingering kiss,
To them it was all the beauty everyone sees,
No sound was heard, but the whispering trees
Beneath the tree with cheese and wine,
Two people sat in this dream of mine.
I knew then just how it would be
When we got together my love and me.
The day would be sunny, quiet and warm
And we would be walking arm in arm,
Then we'd sit with his/her hand in mine
To talk about love, with cheese and wine.

Mary Burroughs

GROWING OLD

On this dull and dreary day
As I sit and pass the time away
There's nothing much but rain and mud
And it don't do us old folk much good

Sitting locked behind closed doors
Tired and shattered from all our chores
Visitors are far and few between
And a smiling face is seldom seen

I just sit here in the cold
Reminiscing of times of old
Thinking of happy times gone past
Trying to smile until the last
Thinking of times when I were strong and bold
Ay'e lad it's a sad life when you're growing old.

B A Smyth

FRIENDSHIP

Friendship is a bond
That holds you both together
Friendship is a trust
That's meant to last forever
Friendship is a jewel
That's precious and so rare
Friendship's when two people
Learn how to show they care
Friendship is a shoulder
That's there for you to cry on
Friendship is a tower of strength
You know you can rely on
Friendship is a special love
That stays until the end
Friendship should be treasured
I'm glad that you're my friend.

Bev Goodridge

THE PLOUGHMAN

So early in the morning,
When times were very lean,
A ploughman worked from the dawning,
To feed, water, and dress his team,
Bridles, collars and traces,
Curricome, brushing, to shine,
Tails, manes, braided with laces,
Brasses, and ribbons, buckled so fine.

In his pocket, shutknife, shilling and string,
A few flat washers to take up play,
Colter to skieth, whipline to fling,
Plug to ploughpoint, silt on clay.
'Oh walk along my beauties,'
'Oh walk along with me',
We've just got an acre to plough today,
Before we go home to tea.

Chained to the horsetrees, false line set,
Furrow side filly, trying hard to buck,
We are yoked up now, real pulling to be met,
'Cuppa Cuppa Bonny, Kit Kat Giddy up'
Hooves now to the earth in full.
Furrows drawn straight and long,
Foaming mouths, clicking, nashing teeth,
Chests and forelegs, stalwart so strong.

As the ground be his table,
The fen dyke reed be his chair,
'Dockie' packed by old Mabel,.
Washed down by weak mild beer.
'My Bonny's coat is like velvet'
'My Kits', the line horse you seem
We have ploughed a full acre today my boys
Now we go home for tea.

Robert Willson

HAPPY WANDERER

When I'm gone think no more of me,
For I'm in the place I want to be,
Wandering o'er the hills and dales,
In the sun, wind and gales,
Free as a bird in flight on air,
Up in the sky so blue and clear,
To meet friends old and new,
They will keep helping me through,
Doing things I wanted to do in life,
But without all the struggle and strife,
Seeing nature at its best,
All the animals full of zest.
Money worries are no more,
That used to make life a bore,
Bills and taxes make me upset,
A flutter in my heart then I'd get,
But all this I have left behind,
Giving me a perfect peace of mind,
So all carry on with lives so bright,
Knowing that I am really alright.

Clem Fletcher

WHO WILL TELL ME?

Three and ten decades
It was written
Flying bullets we'd all be bitten
All the people in our streets
All marching to the same beats
What are we supposed to do?
Who will tell me?
And who told you?
The frantic killer
His eyes all red
Humans upstairs, shivering in their bed
The frail old man
With a life time in his face
Once an important part of our race
The cry of a baby
Has life begun
Or the sound of a pistol and thine will be done
What are we supposed to do?
Who will tell me?
And who told you?
The sound of laughter
Flies through the air
Followed by death because he doesn't care
A thin small child is holding a gun
Defending her right
To die in fun
Are we able to live as one?
Or will we end
Basking in a nuclear sun?

N V Hepworth

THE COUNTRYSIDE

See that tree over there
Is it common or is it rare
Is it yellow or is it green
Such a beauty I've never see
It stands so wide, bold and high
Its branches nearly reaching the sky
The land around so green and pleasant
Look there goes a passing pheasant
Isn't mother nature a wonderful thing
It makes you want to dance and sing
Why do the birds all fly away
But return again another day
the sly old fox that loves to raid
Hens from a henhouse before they've laid
I see you flower so pretty and blue
Is it alright if I talk to you
I'll not pick you because you'll die
You don't want that neither do I
Look after nature it's all we've got
Please don't destroy it preserve the lot.

A McLaughlin

APRON STRINGS

Will you soon be here my child to face the world so new?
Will it hold peace and mystery we all cherish just for you?
Our plans and our dreams we will build for you
Oh bundle of delight!
May love and joy come with you my child
When you steal to us in the night.

Will you still be there my lad
When your boyhood dreams you share?
When all the prizes are given
My dear son will you be there?
Will we be deeply proud for you
When acclaim and degrees you win?
We will be at your side my dear
To guard you from harm and sin?

Will we still be there my son when your bride for life you choose?
Will we be radiantly happy on the day your heart you will lose?
Will she be at your side my love to share your grief and your joy
Will you be at *her* side my love
To smile on the face of *your* boy?

Will you still be there my son when silver tints our hair?
Our dreams for you all fulfilled and complete
When life for you all is so fair
We have surely done our best my son,
May love and peace be yours,
Go on your way my beloved boy
We'll be near - but we will be there!

Wendy Steele

THE MAN WITH NO NAME

I look at you from afar,
Lovely man in your big black car
I know we'll never ever meet
But all I know is I think you're sweet,

Are you married, divorced or single,
I know that you make my spine tingle,
At night I lay awake in my bed
And wonder who'll be stroking your head
Is she pretty, short or tall
Do you give her your everything and all
Or are you lonely just like me
Oh how I wish we two could be
Together for just one tender night
But I'll lay here lonely until morning light

I'd love to look into your eyes
To see love in them, but it wouldn't be wise
To feel your warm breath upon my skin,
Flesh against flesh, lips to lips, a sign for us to begin
A wondrous journey of loving each other,
But I know your love must be for another.

For while you pass my way each day
I can think of loving things I'd like to say,
To the man in dark glasses, and the darkest hair
If only one night of passion to share

So now my secret love I cherish
Knowing I can never have my special wish,
To the man with no name, I love so much
I dream each night of your tender touch,
So just think sometimes of this lonely woman,
Who dreams alone, and is in love with just one man.

Sheila McKie

GOLDEN DAYS

Silent hills and naked trees
Not a sign of flowers or bees
Quiet calm, a sudden gust
Frozen sludge and then grey dust

This is winter so I'm told
It comes soon after autumn gold
No one likes it, it is doom
With not a spark to lift the gloom

Wait though, could all this be wrong
In the park a happy throng
Run and shout and laugh and cheer
Of the cold they show no fear

And over there a robin sings
As now and then the church bell rings
The sun though weak sends down a ray
To make frost glisten and look gay

Perhaps the trees and hills are glad
To rest from summer, when they had
No peace from people, cars and noise
And constant bruising from small boys

God must have known their need to rest
And all his creatures gain their quest
To store up energy to take
A good long rest and then awake

So look on winter as a time
When really life is quite sublime
Cherish the many silent ways
It shows you really golden days

Jean Campbell

ENGLAND'S HERITAGE

A new year has begun again
The old one gone before
As now we look toward new life
For spring comes round once more.
The frost and snow has melted now
Cold rain from forests drip
Upon the life remaining there
In trees and hedgerows tips
But soon new life emerges again
As buds and blossoms grow
Warm sun to make birds' feathers shine
As love for them doth glow.
to make their nests for young to brood
To nurture and protect!
From those who destroy, what nature intends
With hands that wield the axe.
The tall and graceful trees come down
Still dressed in summer green.
As one by one they fall and die
Struck by hands unseen.
What must the 'migrants' feel we ask
As empty space they see.
To fly the miles - cross desert sands
Find England's heritage
Is now destroyed - where once it stood
Where, will they go from here.
But winter is the stepping stone
That takes us into spring
The cherry tree will flower again
At dawn the birds will sing.

Irene Siviour

FROM THE CRADLE TO THE GRAVE

A babe is born, the little one
        Brings tears of joy to all,
And very soon the baby has grown
        Into a child so tall.

School days seem to go so quick,
        And without a word of warning
She's now a gorgeous, teenage chick,
        Fresh as the dew of the morning.

Lovelorn youth now swarm like bees
        To take her hand in marriage,
Now she is a blushing bride
        Within a horse-drawn carriage.

Soon come roses to her cheeks
        As her motherly arms unfurl
Around a little bundle of joy;
        Her very own precious pearl.

But all too soon poor 'Grandmama'
        Is silver-haired and frail,
With pain in her eyes, and ache in all hearts
        The years have told their tale,

Sadly now the time has come
        To say a last *goodbye*,
Her body now an empty shell,
        As life has passed her by.

Sarah Blackburn

CAPTAIN HARRY CLAYTON

I've found my Uncle Harry, I never knew I had,
But I'm so glad to find him, my Grandma's youngest lad.
My Mother Jane was eldest, she'd other brothers too,
Then came Uncle Harry, the youngest of the crew.

Mother died when I was five, Uncle Harry had gone to war,
And so I never knew of him, and me he never saw.
They sent him out to India, and all thro Burma too,
I I could have been so proud of him, but of him I never knew.

Until I heard a cousin say, he'd brought our Uncle home,
He'd brought him back to Huddersfield, cause now he lived alone.
And so I went to see this man, I never knew existed,
And as I walked into the room, I felt that I'd been twisted.

This Captain Harry Clayton, that I had never known,
Held his arms out to me, at last he had come home.
I go to see him every week, in 'Lascelles Hall' Nursing Home,
We know we've lost a lifetime, but now he's not alone.

He tells me of my Mother, how she wrote poetry too.
Things I'd never known of her, things that he only knew.
How Thursday was always baking day, how their Mother made the bread
And how it smelt so lovely, those large crisp leaves, he said.

I sit in such amazement, and hear of those long dead.
Things that I would never have known, till dear Uncle Harry said.
We have not long together, he's eighty five, and frail,
We just hold hands and wonder, at this very sad long tale.

It seems so sad a lifetime passed, and never knew each other
But I'm so glad I found him, Mother's only living brother.
So I'd like to immortalise, this Uncle Harry of mine
And put his name forever in the annals of time.

Kathleen Pogson

THE BOXER

There he was in the ring standing on his own
Sitting at the ringside was his best friend Frank Malone
The crowd went wild as he smiled
The cameras focused on a child

As the opponent entered the ring
The ding of the bell made me ting
He punched a left jab then a right
His friend on the ringside shouted fight

Then the opponent fell on the floor
Was he dead I wasn't sure
The ref counted five was he alive
He was only young it seemed like fun

The crowd cheered as the bell rang
He must have won the other man's down
The lights were flashing as bright as day
Now it's time for the judges' say.

John Woods

NOVEMBER POPPIES

November was cold and windy and I travelled into town,
My head started aching and I was feeling very down.
I'd caught another cold which might easily turn to 'flu,
Still I needn't stay out very long I'd not got much to do.
Then outside Marks and Spencers something made me stop and stare,
For on that cold and wintry afternoon, sat an old man on a chair.
A row of polished medals proudly pinned upon his chest,
His clothes were old and shabby and clearly past their best.
A white stick and dark glasses and a beret on his head,
And on his lap he held a box of poppies brightly red.
His guide dog sat beside him, who looked as old as he,
As people hurried past him with eyes that did not see.
And yet I felt that somehow he was looking straight at me . . .
Embarrassed I walked over to take a poppy from his tray.
And dropped some coins into his tin and turned to walk away,
The self-pity I felt earlier made me ashamed and yet . . .
As he handed me a poppy he said 'lest we forget'
'Bless you miss for your kindness'
His words cut into me.
That he who sacrificed so much,
Was actually thanking me!

Linda Gardner

HEART BREAK HOUSE

It's just a short walk
To the land of despair
Where the tears won't stop falling
And the pain's really there.
It's a heartache away.
But it doesn't take long.
It's for people forgotten.
It's for things that go wrong.
The door's always open.
You can just step inside
With a broken up feeling
That you just cannot hide.
There are lots you can talk to
People aching with pain.
But they'll maybe not hear you
Or remember your name.
Yes it's just a short walk
Come on in, take my hand,
No I don't come here often
Share my hurt, understand.

Jennie Barwell

SORRY

O no, you've noticed I'm another leaflet,
And I've landed on your mat,
But please don't screw me up, and throw me at your cat
Please give me half a chance,
And read what I've got to say,
You never know you might like it
I might even make your day

I'm not offering you riches,
Far more than you could stand,
Or a flashy car
Or a luxury house in a foreign land

I can see from your expression,
You're interest's fading fast,
I'd better tell you my purpose,
Before caring you've gone past.

Well here's the simple truth of it,
An invitation I'll extend,
You guessed it, I'm from next door,
Let's shake hands, forget the argument, and be good friends.

D Freegard

DAY'S END

When the sun sinks in the west,
And all the birds have gone to rest,
When soft warm breezes fill the air
And summer scents are everywhere,
In gardens filled with fruit and flower
Result of many a patient hour
Of happy toil and tender care
In my garden! In the evening, I'll be there!

Of failures I have had my share,
But now there's time to stand and stare,
To pause and listen, hearing sounds
That pressures of the world have drowned
Throughout the heat of a long day.
To watch, reflect, and while I stay,
Cherish such moments while I may.
And who is there to say me 'Nay'?

In my garden in the evening,
All alone with no one there
Peace and quietude around me
Solitude that is so rare
I throw away those cares of day.
My pleasure taken in the way
The world slips quietly into night,
As so must I. Sweet dreams! Sleep tight!

Edith Gaskin

PESTS

Pester me again today
I just can't take no more,
You kids are driving me insane,
You've dirtied all my floor,
Go pester someone else can't you,
Go find a little job or two,
Or maybe take a long long hike,
better still take your bike,
I know I am your mother
But that doesn't mean to say
I might have had enough sometime
I may just go away,
Go pester someone else can't you.
Go to your dad I think he's due,
He's busy yes, but he won't mind,
He likes being pestered he's that kind,
Don't worry too much if he says 'go away'
He only really wants to play.
You're back so soon from pestering dad
What's up loves you look quite sad,
He didn't want to know today,
He told you both to go away,
That's not fair the mean, mean man,
Never mind sweethearts,
Come on and pester your mam.

A Brown

THANKS

I've scrubbed and I've cooked and I've cleaned that big mat
I've polished and ironed and did things like that
Now I've done all these things so I'll just sit a while
But these thoughts in my head
Don't make me want to smile
Do the kids even notice just how tired I am
Or am I just that old woman
you know just their mam.
But then did I notice the things my mum did
I don't think I ever noticed if she was short of a quid.
Now I've time on my hands
Time to think of these things
My mum was an angel who didn't have wings
So before it's too late and the time slips away
I remember these things mum each night and each day
What I now do for them you once did for us
Without ever a grumble without ever a fuss
Thanks mum.

Sarah Anne Turner

UNTITLED

On some sunny distant shore
Waves come tumbling ever more
To look across the open sea
The feeling of happiness and of glee
That at last we can have a rest
This holiday should be one of the best
For us it cannot be too long
The birds fly over with a song
Of joy and happiness
Wind on our faces gently caress
All too soon it comes to an end
It's back to reality we must blend
To face our tasks whatever new
Awaiting for us however few
Maybe next year as we get older
We will stay longer be bolder
That for us so much work
Duties we will be allowed to shirk
Looking back we've done our share
Time for us to stop and stare
At the younger one who
Now have the work to do.

Joye

THE GREAT INDOORS

I think I will make a garden
For a start I need a hedge,
It would be nice for privacy
From the eyes of Flo and Reg,
Conifers are my best bet,
Their growth is quite keen,
I will trim them when they reach the height
When I cannot be seen,
Next I will lay a fine lawn
And try to keep it neat,
I shall buy a hover mower
And cut it twice a week,
Now do I need a greenhouse
Or shall I build a shed,
Where shall I have the rockery
And a lovely flower bed?
I would like a cottage garden
With shrubs that grow so tall,
Maybe I will have a fish pond
And build a dry stone wall,
My garden is now taking shape
But I must stay indoors,
The English summer has arrived
It never rains, just pours!

Janet Bedford

STREET LIFE

Curl up in my box on this cold wintry night
praying for the dawn
longing for the light
All I want is a home
With my very own door
I can't think of anything
        I could want more
A door I could lock
        With my very own key
A key that belonged
        especially to me
Feet flying past
People rushing to their jobs.
Noise of the traffic
        They don't hear my sobs
day slowly dawning
A brand new morning
but it's still just as wet
and it's still just as cold
and all I can do is sit and grow old.

Molly Prince

A SPECIAL DAY

The 'date' in July was on the agenda,
So much joy, it gives to remember,

A day with you both . . . we had waited so long,
No! I won't spoil it dears, and burst into song!

Your holiday home, down by the river.
How lovely for you, to use all the summer,

Lots of chatting and plenty of tea,
Where do we start! There is so much to see,

The kitchen and bedroom, bathroom as well,
Then into the lounge . . . my isn't this swell!

The view is superb, as the boats go by,
We sit and we gaze, with a contented sigh,

Then of we go, to explore some more,
A walk by the river, we found 'bargains galore',

Yes lots of 'goodies', on the Lifeboat stall,
We bought some presents for one and all!

On to the 'island', a lovely long walk,
In the warm sun, we just stroll, and we talk,

Back to your 'Haven', it's now time for dinner,
Such scrumptious food, won't help us get thinner!

Our last cup of tea, at the end of the day,
To you dear friend, what more can I say?

We have loved every minute and don't want to go,
Some day to return . . . *please* just let us know.

E Nye

BIRDS

What a wonderful sight
to see and hear birds sing.
At early morn they chirp and delight
Us with the wonder of nature.
And what is their structure,
So tiny, no matter what the weather
Rain, or shine, you'll see them together
having a great time.
Just look out of your window
And watch them flying to and fro.
It's a wonderful world
If only we all thought so.
Nature is at its best
When birds fly and nest.
The moral of this little verse
Is to appreciate the little things
On this earth,
And realise the joy it brings.

Lilian Marks

WASH

Wash to revive the spirit that was once here
To dissolve away all uncertainties and fears.
Wash to wipe away the fog so I can clearly see
To scrape away the mud and blood to show the real me.
Wash to cleanse deep down so that confidence grows
To help open the doors that were once closed
　　　　Simply wash.

Hayley Singlehurst

TO CHRISTINE

Blessed little one year old
On this your special day
Within our arms may we enfold
You and by our actions say
What we in words cannot express
With hearts so full as ours
Since by your very presence bless
All our waking hours

Christmas comes but once each year
We're glad it does so too
Why did you choose Christmas dear
To let your teeth come through?
No longer will your toothless grin
Greet us each new morn
No wonder you're so pale and thin
Staying up 'til dawn.

You'd probably choose your birthday but
It's just one day per annum
There's lots more toothy pegs to cut
We hope of course you've had 'em
How nice when you begin to walk
But you're just a little lazy
There is no hurry yet to talk
You'll drive is both plumb crazy.

Happy precious little girl
Who did our hopes fulfil
In our shell you are a pearl
On our cake the frill
We wish you joy untold today
And throughout the year
One more thing we'd like to say
Happy Birthday dear

Walter Leslie Arnold

TALE OF A DYING SPECTRUM

In my youth I once was red,
happy, young and free.
Then, when I was yellow,
thoughts were born to me.

In indigo I was stronger
In purple stronger still
In blue my life was longer
In green I was over the hill.

Now that I am old and grey,
Soon I will be black.
Then white, I'll simply fade away,
All colour I will lack.

Alexander Southgate (13)

GOOD RIDDANCE

That taste of twist
That smell of dust
That jet-black hole
My father cussed
At last has gone,
And gone for good,
Like many a miner
'Neath a cross of wood
So think on this, all those who cry,
At least no other man will die
To win black gold,
And show true grit,
In a workplace
Aptly named - *The Pit*

Denzil Broadstock

THE WHELKS

The tide is out we'll head for the beach
Looking for whelks just in our reach
It's bitterly cold and our hands are blue
Some of the whelks seem to stick like glue
We pull the seaweed aside
Under which they seem to hide
We have to uncover this mass of black shells
We pick fast to fill our pails
Grovelling in the puddles
Cracking the seaweed with the little bubbles
Empty the pails into the sack
Now we are beginning to feel our sore back
Been such a lovely healthy day
Now we wonder what they will pay
Light a fire to get a heat
Round it now we'll have a seat
It's time we were making tracks
Hoist the sacks upon our backs
The tide's coming in
Hardly tell where we have been
We found plenty of whelks
All that remains is to carry our bulks.

Marie Foulis Kennedy

THE WAVES

When the air is clear,
And the day is still,
Then the little waves
Sing a soft song.
A murmuring, tinkling,
Swishing song.
Dribbling forward,
Drawing back.
Hardly moving the sand.

But when the wind is wild,
Freezing man and child,
Then the waves are
Capped with spray.
Thundering, roaring,
Snarling, swishing,
Swirling pebbles
Around rock pools,
Pounding the cliffs round the bay.

The tide comes in and
The tide goes out.
The waves wash to and fro'.
Ever forward, ever backward,
Burbling as they go.
Chuckling, sighing,
Leaping, dying,
Scattering a mist of spray
As they dash towards the shore.

Marjorie Sellick

UNTITLED

Is that a green shoot I can see
In my back garden bare,
Or are my eyes deceiving me
No, there's another there.

I think I'll take a good look round
Now I can clearly see
That buds are forming everywhere
On every bush and tree.

And what's this wriggling at my feet
A big fat juicy worm,
I know they do the garden good
But 'ooh' they make me squirm.

If this is springtime,. give me more
Warm sun and cool breeze blowing
Of course there is a drawback
The grass will now need mowing.

B Webber

THANKSGIVING

I live within a troubled world
Of wars, corruption, greed;
And though I have a humble life
I'm rich in things I need.

I count my blessings every day
And know I've peace of mind.
My prayers are offered, Lord, to soothe
The troubles of mankind.

I'm ever truly grateful
For living on this earth.
With such beauty all around me
I thank thee for my birth.

And now I've reached my senior years
My life I really treasure,
For as each day goes 'racing' by,
I memorise with pleasure.

I think of all the friendships.
Of the love and joys I've seen,
I render my thanksgiving, Lord,
Oh, how happy I have been.

Mollie A Bally

TO SCRUFFY

This is dedicated to my very best friend,
Sadly his life has now come to an end,
He was always there, with a wag of a tail,
Making me happy, he never did fail.

Now he's left me, I feel all alone,
No squeaky toys, no old dogs bone.
No coming to bed with me every night,
No lying beside me, eyes shining bright.

You could not suffer, I let you go
But I loved you so much, I am sure that you know
If I could have you back for a day
We'd go for a walk, in the fields we would play.

I left you there, and said goodbye
I knew that you were going to die
I stroked your coat, your nose I kissed
You'll never know how much you're missed

You were so much more than a pet to me,
Because you were my very best friend don't you see
Always so happy to see me come home
But now you're gone and I feel all alone.

So now you've gone where the good doggies go,
You know I'll always love you so
So be a good boy in whatever you do
And remember always how much I love you.

Alison Pye

ODE TO UNCLE PETER'S RETIREMENT

No more early mornings in the dark
Or breakfast taken with the lark
You will be able to take it easy
Do things when you like, not at all if you're queasy!

No more desks, paper or pens
Plenty of time now for making friends
No more 'passes' at the dockyard gate
Plenty more time now - you can be late

Sit back and relax now start to enjoy
Things you've not done since you were a boy
Fishing, biking, a hobby or two
The choice is yours it's up to you.

Don't forget though to help with those chores
Not just outside but also indoors
Learning to cook - it can be such fun
But clear up the kitchen once you're done!

Enjoy yourself - learn to relax
Forget the office and the fax
Concentrate energy on your sea scouts
Messing about in all these boats.

Every week you'll go out sailing
Helping cadets with lots of bailing
The days will pass and before too long
A month has passed and nothing's gone wrong.

Now your final working week is here
All your colleagues will shed a tear
But think how envious they must be
Not just them, 'cos so are we.

We think you'll be pleasantly surprised
How well you'll adjust to your new demise
Shopping together, on the moors for a day
It's so much better than work - anyday!

S Hancock

BOXGROVE MAN

Oh Roger, Roger, you're so old,
Half a million years I'm told.
First European, six feet three,
Found at Boxgrove, near to me.

When monstrous creatures stalked the earth
That was the moment of your birth,
You roamed the forests all around
What now we call the Sussex Downs.

Thirteen stones of muscled man,
You learned to hunt in hostile land.
Sub-tropical, as it was then,
Malevolent to beasts and men.

Primeval man, what destiny
Decreed your bone's discovery?
Oh was it chance, or was it plan
That we discovered Boxgrove Man?

Oh Roger, Roger, where was I,
An atom floating in the sky?
We never met, how could it be?
I know of you, but you not me!

Jacqui Rochford

INFORMATION

We hope you have enjoyed reading this book - and that you will continue to enjoy it in the coming years.

If you like reading and writing poetry drop us a line, or give us a call, and we'll send you a free information pack.

Write to

Anchor Books Information
1-2 Wainman Road
Woodston
Peterborough
PE2 7BU.